Finding Ghosts in Phoenix

Katie Mullaly and J. Patrick Ohlde

Photography by
Mikal Mullaly

Schiffer
Publishing Ltd®

4880 Lower Valley Road, Atglen, Pennsylvania 19310

Other Schiffer Books by Katie Mullaly and J. Patrick Ohlde:
Scare-Izona: A Travel Guide to Arizona's Spookiest Spots, 978-0-7643-2844-2, $14.95
Tucson's Most Haunted, 978-0-7643-3153-4, $14.99

Other Schiffer Books on Related Subjects:
Ghosts of Central Arizona, 978-0-7643-3387-3, $14.99
Southern Arizona's Most Haunted, 978-0-7643-3416-0, $14.99

Designed by "Sue"
Type set in Grasshopper/NewBskvll BT

ISBN: 978-0-7643-3583-9
Printed in the United States of America

Schiffer Books are available at special discounts for bulk purchases for sales promotions or premiums. Special editions, including personalized covers, corporate imprints, and excerpts can be created in large quantities for special needs. For more information contact the publisher:

Published by Schiffer Publishing Ltd.
4880 Lower Valley Road
Atglen, PA 19310
Phone: (610) 593-1777;
Fax: (610) 593-2002
E-mail: Info@schifferbooks.com

For the largest selection of fine reference books on this and related subjects, please visit our web site at:
www.schifferbooks.com

We are always looking for people to write books on new and related subjects.
If you have an idea for a book please contact us at the above address.

This book may be purchased from the publisher. Include $5.00 for shipping.
Please try your bookstore first.
You may write for a free catalog.

In Europe, Schiffer books are distributed by
Bushwood Books
6 Marksbury Ave.
Kew Gardens
Surrey TW9 4JF England
Phone: 44 (0) 20 8392 8585; Fax: 44 (0) 20 8392 9876
E-mail: info@bushwoodbooks.co.uk
Website: www.bushwoodbooks.co.uk

Contents

Dedications

To Mikal, Seamus, and Liam… You are my favorite people in the world. I love you, MWUA!

~ Katie

▷▷▷▷▷▷▷▷▷▷▷▷

To Mom and Dad… Thank you for all of your love and support and understanding. I couldn't have done any of this without you and I appreciate it more than words could ever express.

~ Patrick

Acknowledgments

† God: As always, for providing an afterlife to begin with.

† Dinah Roseberry and Schiffer Publishing: For giving us the chance to live the dream.

† Summer Disney: For being Patrick's silver lining and all around wonderful.

† Peter Leon: For putting us in movies and helping us with ours. When anyone needs some knots tied, they go to him.

† Mo and Clint: For being our most awesome new members.

† Eric Shumacher: For support, advice, and really bad puns.

† Riyad Kalla: For giving us a place to vent.

† Hazel Redmon: For buying the book even when she didn't need to. Thanks Gran!

† Marian Diggins: For coining the term "Hanging Around Ghost" even if it was just in a dream.

† Jenny Gubernick: For talking us up to librarians who talk us up to her.

† Jenny Wagner: For being cool about Patrick taking time off.

† Jeff Stephenson: For helping Patrick get an awesome job that allows him to keep writing.

† Mark Boccuzzi and Dr. Julie Beischel: For being awesome, letting us rant, and for not lumping us in with "the rest of them."

† Gertrude Schmeidler: For paving the way for everyone who wants to make the paranormal "normal."

† Jaci Vigil: For her enthusiasm and editing superpowers, even when it means she has to sleep with the light on.

† WCGAPS: For taking time to sit and chat with us.

† Alice Jung and Michael Ramos: For giving us the run of the museum.

† Sean Larkin: For his enthusiastic participation and his great ghost stories.

† Keith Jackson: For agreeing to hang out with us in a creepy, dark, haunted bar.

† Diane Stress: For going above and beyond in her support and promotion of us and in the process reminding us why we do this.

† The Wondrous Duck-Billed Platypus: For proving that anything is possible.

We would also like to thank the following people for their vital and thoughtful contributions: Dave Wilson, Steve Ikeda, Jennifer and Kim at Mystic Paper, and Marshall Trimble.

Introduction

Ah, Phoenix... Beautiful city, beautiful people, endless sunshine... At least that is what the board of tourism might mention to anyone planning a visit to the fifth largest city in the United States. While all of that is true, one thing that Phoenix is less inclined to brag about are the various shades, spooks, and specters that amble about in a decidedly sunless haze of post-mortem confusion. Hidden in the darkest corners and deepest recesses of Arizona's golden capital, Phoenix certainly boasts its share of unwanted attention in the form of natural — and sometimes unnatural — deaths, murders, violent crimes, and other stunning examples of gruesome, unexpected, or untimely departing. Now, that is not to say if you live in Phoenix, you will die a horrible death; you are going to die, no matter where you live. It simply stands to reason that, in a city with nearly two million people, the percentage of paranormal activity will be exponentially increased.

As paranormal investigators, we have made it our passion to seek out these bits of legend and lore, research and document them, and — in a sense — bring the dead back to life. In recent years, there has certainly been an increased interest in the study of the paranormal. One need only turn on a television to find such shows as "Ghost Hunters," "Paranormal State," "A Haunting," "Most Haunted," and a myriad of others dedicated in one form or another to the topic of the paranormal. However, in spite of the increased interest in paranormal investigation, it has not necessarily translated into an increased acceptance that there is, in fact, a life beyond the physical world. Religious implications aside, there is an entire community of researchers, investigators, scientists, and sensitives who have experienced, time and time again, phenomena that cannot be explained using any current science or logic, experiences that are at once both tangible and illogical, ethereal and visceral — *experiences that are paranormal.*

We understand that ghosts are scary and nobody wants to live in a haunted house, but why is that? Is it because there is truly something to fear, or is it because we — as corporeal beings — simply misunderstand paranormal activity? There is an interesting dichotomy when it comes to taking sides on the existence of ghosts: Those who are firm believers, and those who claim a staunch disbelief, but cry like babies at the slightest creak of an old floorboard. We suspect that in most cases, "I don't believe in ghosts," actually translates into "I am so terrified of seeing a ghost that the mere mention of ghosts makes me want to pee my pants and curl up into the fetal position." What we have here, folks, is a simple fear of the unknown. Now, just to show our paranormal chops, we've *lived* in haunted houses. We have *seen*, *felt*, and *heard* things. We have awakened to translucent figures standing next to our beds. We have photographed anomalies that are not explainable as normal phenomena. Basically, we know how freaky ghosts can be, but we have simply just stopped being afraid.

Please come with us to visit a few of Phoenix's most well-known haunted locations, as well as some not-so-well-known ghostly hangouts. We'll even sneak you into a few places that are…ahem… officially *not* haunted. As I mentioned, our job is to document and research this stuff for you. We are happy to spend the night in an old, dark mansion so you don't have to. We love the adrenaline rush of seeing a full-body apparition and hearing the hollow din of a disembodied voice. We enjoy the satisfaction that comes with completing even the most daunting investigation, especially when other investigative groups have run from the same building with their tails between their legs. We have a very real passion for investigating, and we very much want to bring about knowledge and acceptance of the paranormal. As we have for many years, we want nothing more than to emphasize the *normal* in paranormal.

Why Phoenix?

Ghosts and paranormal activity can be found pretty much anywhere in the world. Anywhere that people live and die you will find activity of some kind or another. Of course not all locations are created equal. Without knowing exactly what causes paranormal activity, it is hard to conclude definitively why one area is more active than another; however, there does seem to be an increase in activity in those locations that have had a lot of life and death for a really long time. Trauma and violence also seem to contribute to an increased likelihood of activity manifesting, so places that have been populated for long periods of time with an accompanying history of violence tend to have a much better chance of being haunted. Arizona in general and Phoenix in particular have just such a tendency. Founded in 1868 and incorporated as a city in 1881, Phoenix is the capital of the last of the contiguous states to be admitted into the Union. Arizona became a state in 1912 and has gone on to boast a population of 1,552,259 in the city proper and 4,281,899 in the Phoenix Metropolitan area. That is a lot of growth in a relatively short amount of time, but these early settlers to the valley were not the first to reside there.

From around 700 to 1400 CE the area that would become Phoenix was inhabited by the Hohokam, a tribe of Native Americans named by the Akimel O'odham for their departure and subsequent disappearance. During their more than 1,000-year occupation of the area, the Hohokam crafted 135 miles of irrigation canals, which allowed the ground to be able to support crops. It is believed that a drought ending in 1450 caused the Hohokam to leave the area.

It wasn't until Jack Swilling, a veteran of the Civil War, founded the area in 1867 that people would return to the valley. Like many men of the time, Swilling came to the west to seek his fortune in the 1950s and operated mostly out of Wickenburg. Traveling south on an outing, he stopped to rest at the base of the White Tank Mountains. Looking at the valley, he realized it was an area that could support farming and, when he saw the Hohokam canal system cutting paths to the river, he knew he really had something. Swilling had new canals built over the old ones and the settlement sprang up around them. Over the course of the next thirteen years the settlement became a city. Phoenix takes its name from the mythical Phoenix bird, which immolates itself and is reborn. Given its rise from the ashes of a dead civilization as well as the city's heat, the name is apt. It was named state capital upon the state's acceptance into the Union mostly due to its central location. It was smaller at the time than other cities, but it grew exponentially in the decades that followed.

Phoenix tends not to have the same manner of raucous stories of murder and mayhem that some other Arizona cities and towns like Tucson and Tombstone enjoy, but it has seen its share of modern violent crime and unfortunate goings-on. Examples of this range from murders to natural disasters and everything in between and are the kinds of things that tend to lead to paranormal activity.

While not really associated with death in particular, Phoenix hosted a World War II internment camp known as Papago Park Prisoner of War Camp. The "residents" of the camp were German prisoners of war and, as one would imagine, times were not peaches and cream. While there were certain to have been deaths at this camp, just the general negativity from such a place would be more than enough to leave a lasting impression on the location. Few of the buildings remain today, but certainly paranormal activity does not discriminate against the location after the loss of the original building.

On the more grisly side of things, on Thanksgiving night 1942, a riot turned deadly for a number of U.S. troops stationed near Phoenix. Stemming from several troops resisting arrest by the military police, the riot escalated when the troops fled to a particular part of the city and were subsequently surrounded and blocked in by the MPs who then opened fire on civilian homes with a .50 caliber machine gun. As one would expect, many fatalities resulted and led to Army personnel being banned from the city for a time.

As the population grew in Phoenix, so too did the crime, as is generally the case. Organized crime in particular gained a foothold in the city and in 1976 the mob carried out a hit on investigative reporter Don Bolles by car bomb. By the 1980s, street gangs and drug issues became an increasing problem as well as an upsurge in prostitution. As late as 2006, two simultaneous serial killer cases occurred. The Baseline Killer claimed the lives of nine people in addition to committing fifteen rapes and eleven kidnappings between 2005 and 2006. At the same time, the Serial Shooter was operating in Mesa. This killer committed eight murders and was involved in at least twenty-nine other shootings in the area.

Despite the tandem serial murderers, crime has gone down in Phoenix in recent years and the city should not be regarded as a particularly unsafe place to live. Still, with colorful history comes colorful activity and Phoenix has that in spades. Well, it allegedly has it in spades. As you will see, despite years and years worth of reports and storytelling, many locations in Phoenix are tight-lipped about their activity and some flat out deny it. Perhaps it is a fear of being tarnished by some of the more unsavory stories that have come out of Phoenix in the recent past, but many residents and business owners are not eager to share anything that might make them look strange or unsavory. Still, with a depth of history and population like Phoenix, there is bound to be much more activity than some residents are willing to share.

Section One

Navigating a Paranormal Investigation

The members of Wailing Bansidhe Investigations... From left to right: J. Patrick Ohlde, Maureen "Mo" Mullaly, Katie Mullaly, Clint Austin, and Mikal Mullaly.

Chapter One:

Who Are We?

Since paranormal investigating is more esoteric than anything, it's important to throw out the credentials just to make sure that we are not trying to sell you a bill of goods including certification as a triple tarot master graduate of Jim and Skippy's School of Paranormal Mayhem and HVAC Repair.

Collectively, we are — and always have been — Wailing Bansidhe Investigations. We are collectors of information, documenting all things paranormal. While the rest of the paranormal society is busy competing in the "build a better ghost trap" contest, we are the ones recording the minutes. We are the ones you call for reassurance and we are the ones who focus on putting the "normal" back into paranormal. Rather than get embroiled in the ongoing drama of investigator rivalry, we have stepped aside to let the combat-geared paranormal task force run head-long into the cloak-wearing, Middle Earth-worshipping dragon slayers who can also, apparently, see dead people. It will be a collision not unlike the accidental mixing of ammonia with bleach… Stand back, everyone.

So, who are we? Let's take a roll call.

Katie Mullaly

When not engaging in witty repartee, Katie is the unlikely pack leader and protagonist of this ghost story. Having had an interest in ghosts since passage through the birth canal, Katie has made it her focus to read and absorb every piece of information relating to the paranormal and has studied the subject of paranormal psychology under the tutelage of Bill Everist — one of the most well-respected parapsychologists in the field — while attending Pima Community College. Her participation in numerous paranormal investigations has given her irrefutable "street cred," and her increasing impatience with glory-seeking paranormal opportunists has led her to adopt the motto, "Please don't piss on my leg and tell me it's raining."

Mikal Mullaly

Mikal does not believe anything is ever real or that anyone is ever telling the truth under any circumstances. Not surprisingly, if Katie's dead parents floated above him and led him directly to the Holy Grail, which he then exhumed and held within his own hands, he would say, "Whatever... They were totally full of crap." Mikal is also the esteemed photographer, driver, and official troubadour of Wailing Bansidhe.

J. Patrick Ohlde

Just call him Patrick. Please don't try to fuss with the "J." It looks great on the cover of a book, but when addressing him he is Patrick — and he is the official, card-carrying, degree-holding psychology major of the group, giving us substance and in-your-face credibility. Also having studied under the direction of Bill Everist, Patrick is THE MAN when it comes to arguing the validity of paranormal investigating.

Why We Do What We Do

In the past few decades, the world of paranormal investigation has grown exponentially from the days of the delightfully eccentric Ed and Lorraine Warren appearing in the *National Enquirer* (articles that I LOVED reading in my youth) and the handful of parapsychologists brave enough to publicly declare an interest in unexplained phenomena, to a worldwide community of ghost-hunting groups, tours, and television shows replicating faster than a wet mogwai.

While the increased interest in the subject matter is encouraging insofar as those with an interest not being mocked as hatefully or categorized as devil worshippers, the once clear, sparkling, nearly uncharted waters of paranormal investigation have become somewhat muddied and polluted with garbage-spewing groups that favor notoriety over protocol. As a direct result, paranormal groups have developed a tendency to sniff each other out like unwelcome predators, further exacerbating the lack of unity or cohesiveness in the paranormal community.

Smoke and Mirrors

The primary reason that paranormal investigating groups came about was to serve as an outlet for curiosity on the part of the investigator. Through the years, and especially most recently, groups have adopted a continuous shift in their strategies to conform to what the current standard dictates. Now, when we say "current standard," what we are really getting at is "what the group next-door" or — more to the point — "what the group on TV is doing."

In Arizona, we can do a basic Internet search and come back with the names of a dozen or so organizations that claim to be the first group and *the best* group around. With no umbrella organization in place to oversee checks and balances, groups can make a variety of unquantifiable claims in an attempt to posture themselves as the most highly sought after group in the state. Often you will find harmless yet completely unattainable claims such as, "participated in hundreds of investigations," or statements that suggest recent trends in investigating. For example, groups that once touted "great orb captures" now insist all orbs are dust, or groups that claim "only scientific methods," but have no bona fide scientist in the group.

I have also noticed a recent trend towards "we do not use psychics," which is actually unfortunate because one *authentic* psychic can provide a lot more insight than eight hours of audio filled with questionable artifact noise. This is the great "smoke and mirrors" secret of paranormal investigation: it is ninety-nine percent hype and one percent actual investigating. Frankly, we're tired of keeping the big secret, so we are laying all the cards on the table.

It is important to point out that many groups are on the up-and-up. They want to investigate your situation and help you come to some reasonable conclusion about what is going on in your life or in your home that may be causing you to experience what you believe to be paranormal. However, of the groups found during a rudimentary Google search, we know of a couple of "bad apples" that blaze such a trail of destruction that other groups simply roll their eyes at the mere mention of their name. Often, reputable groups will receive "911" emails from homeowners who have been visited by these groups and told any manner of lies involving the nature of their activity. Sometimes leaders of these groups will make suggestions like, "Abandon all your belongings and permanently evacuate your home and don't ever go back." This is a problem because people actually follow this advice, and yes, that event actually happened. These are the whack jobs that we warn you about. Once the damage is done, it is very difficult to clean up the emotional and traumatic mess that is left behind by groups like these, and they are the ones perpetuating the myth that *all* paranormal investigators are bad and crazy.

While we wholeheartedly support the notion of a paranormal Pangaea, and we enjoy opening friendly, productive dialogue with investigators across the board, we absolutely must weed out the groups that bring nothing but inaccuracy and irresponsibility into the mix. Frankly, we have consumed enough of this crap, and we are now full. Game over. We realize that this viewpoint might not win us any "Most Popular Investigator" awards among the good ol' boy network of the paranormal world, but that's only because their wizard is mad that our little dog pulled the curtain back, revealing that these groups are ignorant, dangerous, and totally malignant.

Also we don't really care, since *we* are one of the organizations that really do know what we are talking about. Check the records. We want to keep the playing field even, and allow the wheat to separate from the chaff. If you are in a situation that requires the services of a paranormal investigator, don't just pick the one with the fanciest website — if a group has that much time to spend on a website, they have very little else going on. Please feel free to email us at info@wailingbansidhe. com for a list of recommended and reputable groups.

On the bright side, Wailing Bansidhe Investigations considers itself fortunate to be part of a very tight, very strong community of paranormal investigating groups that are open to welcoming new investigators, but also not afraid to vet out the loons. We have to draw the line somewhere. So many well-intended groups have taken on the daunting task of attempting to find irrefutable proof of the existence of ghosts, and it is a very hard row to hoe. For as many groups that wish to find the one compelling video or indisputable EVP, there are ten people who want to tear down their theories or findings as unmitigated bunk, going as far as calling the investigators stupid and suggesting they get "real jobs" and stop lying to the world and stealing its hard-earned dollars. We fully support the dignified study of the existence of an afterlife, but since we do not need convincing, we have chosen to focus on the full gestalt of the investigation rather than just the validity of the findings. Often, it is the experience itself that is most compelling rather than just a "check yes or no" statistical elimination.

What we want to convey, most of all, is that absolutely anyone can participate in a paranormal investigation. You do not need an advanced degree in quantum physics or a ridiculously hyper-developed clairvoyance. There is enough paranormal activity happening in the world that there is something for everyone to experience and — once you know what you are looking for — the intensity of it can make you change your whole belief system and, occasionally, your underpants. Since our goal is to bring the process of paranormal investigation to everyone, we will use only methods that can be learned easily and performed without public scrutiny. We will use easily attainable and affordable tools, and we will not claim any special powers or perform any bizarre incantations or instruct the reader to "call the corners." We want to share our experiences with our readers and provide them with an easy-to-read road map for self-guided ghost hunting.

Our Methodology

There are almost as many different methodologies out there for paranormal investigating as there are paranormal investigators. These range all over the spectrum from super scientific to super spiritual. At the end of the day, it all comes down to intentions and education.

Anyone can investigate the paranormal, but it helps a great deal if that person takes steps to learn how to do it. Choosing the right methodology generally comes down to your goals and personal preferences. If you are the kind of person who is very technology-oriented and likes to do statistics, then you might take on a method that favors computers and high-tech equipment. If you are the kind who likes to go with your feelings or fancy yourself a sensitive, there are other types of methods to cater to that as well. The vagaries of those methods will be discussed later, but because of our particular goals — helping people determine whether or not they are crazy and cataloging ghost stories — we have chosen a modified version of a method typically known as Sensory Replication.

As a concept, Sensory Replication is essentially trying to reproduce the reported activity without any knowledge of that activity. You go in to the location "blind," which means you have no knowledge of the activity or history of the location. You map out a floor plan of the place and perform a walk-through of each of the locations on the map. The walk-throughs are performed one at a time and you are not permitted to speak to anyone else until everyone has completed their trip. Even when the gag order is lifted, any communication regarding results or impressions of the walk-through is a no-no.

The goal is to try to replicate the reported activity, so you spend time in each room or location and take note of what you experience there. If you go into a room and a particular part of the room makes you feel dizzy or light-headed, you mark the spot on the floor plan and write what you felt. I typically number the Xs and write my impressions in list form below the map just to keep it tidy.

If you are spending the night at the location, the "after" walk-through time involves basically going back to your room or sleeping bag on the floor and trying to go to sleep. If you stay up for whatever reason, it is important that you not talk to anyone about your impressions. During sleepy time, you should always keep a dream journal. Sometimes dreams can contain very powerful experiences. It seems a little silly, but it can be very valid. I doubted this when I first started investigating until I had an encounter with a former manager at the bed and breakfast in which I was staying. She came up to me in my dream and introduced herself and it occurred to me in the dream that I shouldn't be meeting a pretty lady in a white nightgown, and startled awake. Upon relaying the story to my mentor Bill Everist, I found that not only did I have the correct name for the former manager of the B&B and the correct physical description, I was also the third person to have the same exact dream — and I was not the last. Apparently the room was formerly her office and she returns from beyond the grave to make visitors feel welcome. Now that is what I call customer service and, as you can see, keeping dream journals is every bit as important as writing down impressions on the walk-through.

During the investigation there should never be — *under any circumstances* — alcohol or drugs used by team members. Any altered state of consciousness will invalidate all the findings and will most likely result in the inebriated party embarrassing themselves in a way to cause *no* paranormal groups to ever again return. There are those who believe that using substances like peyote or LSD will open the mind and allow the user to see things on some other level. The problem with that is that you cannot discern between a legitimate experience and a drug-induced trip through the looking glass. For valid results, an investigator must be completely sober and drug free at all times.

Guerrilla Ghost Hunting

As we've just stated, the type of paranormal investigation that we practice is something of a modified and truncated sort. We are not interested in the hard core statistic gathering and scientific journal writing. We also aren't terribly keen on managing large groups of people and juggling their schedules while making sure all of their delicate sensibilities are being nurtured along the process of psychic self-discovery and personal growth. We also really hate having to coordinate large-scale investigations and all that entails. There is a reason that there are only three of us (although we did recently add an unprecedented TWO new members) and why we chose the sort of ghost hunting we do, a kind we affectionately refer to as "Guerrilla Ghost Hunting."

When you say something like Guerrilla Ghost Hunting, it may conjure up images of Arnold Schwarzenegger chasing an alien through the jungle at best and Ned Beatty squealing like a pig at worst, but think of it more in context of filmmaking than armed combat. The term in films refers to a practice of by-the-seat-of-your-pants filmmaking that involves an outside-the-system methodology. Filmmakers who do this typically work on small budgets and use things they have on hand. They also tend to sneak into places and steal shots, which is *not* something our approach encourages. We are really just taking the spirit of the practice with us. What it means to us is that we are not going to invest a ton of money on equipment, vehicles, or other such expenses. It can be done as a hobby without rigorous time commitment. Because we aren't trotting out a preponderance of equipment, we can visit public places casually and perform an unobtrusive walk-through even in places where we aren't officially authorized to investigate. All of this comes with some healthy caveats, of course.

First of all, when we talk about investigating places that we aren't authorized to investigate, we are not talking about trespassing — *that is a HUGE no-no.* It will get you arrested and tossed in jail, and we are not going to help bail you out or be held responsible in any way for your lack of judgment. Just so that is clear. When you investigate, be it in a professional capacity or a less formal capacity, you should always be respectful and discreet. If you don't call first for official permission to investigate, then you should understand that you will not have the same access you would enjoy with a sanctioned visit. You have to restrict your moves to the common areas that anyone can go into, and you don't want to pull a bunch of scary-looking tools out of your pockets like you are doing some kind of hazmat sweep or radiation testing.

Also, this does not mean that you can be sloppy with your methods. Just because you are not going to publish in any journals does not mean you should just wander the place taking random pictures and sloppily throwing notes on some paper and then proclaim the place is super active. That doesn't do anyone any good, particularly when you get on Internet message boards to try to do battle with skeptics over your "evidence." They will eat you alive and you will have done the heavy lifting for them. Whatever methods you choose, you should be as thorough and complete as possible. Always look for confounds, never show up drunk or high, and don't act like a jackass.

We went over our preferred method of investigating, Sensory Replication, in the previous section, but that is not the only game in town. When cautioning others on what not to do, sometimes instructions on what to do become lost in the shuffle. We feel, given our more casual approach, that Sensory Replication is the best investigation method for the Guerrilla Ghost Hunting model, but that doesn't mean it is the only one you should use.

Some people are very interested in the technology end of things and feel that they need to capture some manner of evidence on a device to feel satisfied. That is a fine approach if that is where your interest lies. There is a myriad of equipment to choose from when ghost hunting, but they're not all created equal. Some pieces are definitely better than others and, when you put it in the context of Guerrilla Ghost Hunting, the conversation gets that much more complicated because you have the added considerations of ease of use, unobtrusiveness and discretion, occupation of physical space, and simple matters of convenience to issues already present, such as "does this thing do anything at all that it claims to?"

The first rule of thumb, and it is kind of obvious, is you should stick to equipment that is easy to carry in some cargo pants or a messenger bag and that you can hold in one hand. As mentioned earlier, showing up with a full proton pack strapped to your back while you uncoil four hundred feet of cable to connect to your elaborate computer and video camera bank is probably missing the point a bit and will have you kicked from the place faster than you can say, "but on TV…"

Always keep in mind that places of business are just that — if business cannot be done in a reasonable way because of your shenanigans, then not only will you be ejected, but more than likely that location will treat future investigators like they have leprosy. No one wants a location to be harmed by investigating and no one wants to see them take an anti-ghost hunting policy. You may not think about it at the time, but you are ambassadors for the whole of the community when you investigate, so keep it small, light, and unobtrusive. There are a few specific pieces of equipment that will serve you well here.

EMF Detector

Electromagnetic Field (EMF) is basically just a physical field that surrounds any objects charged with electricity. Your toaster, DVR, cell phone, breaker box, TV, computer, and even the Easy Bake Oven all give off such fields, as does anything that operates from electricity. The EMF detector does just what it sounds like: it detects the fields and shows their intensity by way of a flashing light and beeping sound.

Unless you are particularly fond of beeping sounds, we recommend you keep that function turned off and just go with the light.

You may be thinking "so that is nifty, but what does it mean to ghost hunting?" It is believed that discarnate spirits also give off their own EMF, which can be detected and graded by this piece of equipment. As with most equipment, there is debate regarding the veracity of claims that EMF detectors can be used to pick up on the electromagnetic fields of ghosts — as well as if ghosts emit them in the first place.

If you pursue ghost hunting, it will soon become obvious that most equipment in the field is used like circumstantial evidence as opposed to a collector of hard facts. It can generally point you in the right direction, but it doesn't necessarily prove anything. In the case of the EMF detector, you tend to look for spikes in the fields in places where no field should exist. For instance, if you are walking around a room and are not near anything electrical, which can be difficult in and of itself, and it starts flashing quickly (or "buries the needle," as they say in the movie "Ghostbusters"), then you might have some ghost activity in that area.

Obviously the first step is to make sure that there is nothing mundane that can be causing the spike. Check to find out if the floor or ceiling might have a line of wires running through it or make sure you don't have anything on you, like your cell phone, that could be causing the spikes. If you are using the dongle attachment, make sure it isn't too close to the EMF detector itself as this could cause a false spike. You should also make sure that the batteries in the unit itself are fresh or you could get some erratic behavior from it that way.

Once a general absence of an alternate explanation is established, the best way to proceed with the device is to ask questions and request an answer on your detector. Now this is a bit sketchy because even though an entity might emit an electromagnetic field, there is no guarantee that it can manipulate it in any meaningful way. However, if you ask something to flash once for yes and twice for no and then ask a series of questions and get appropriate responses, it seems unlikely that a static source of electricity such as another device would be causing the results. If there is some kind of rhyme or reason behind the responses or the activity on the detector, you

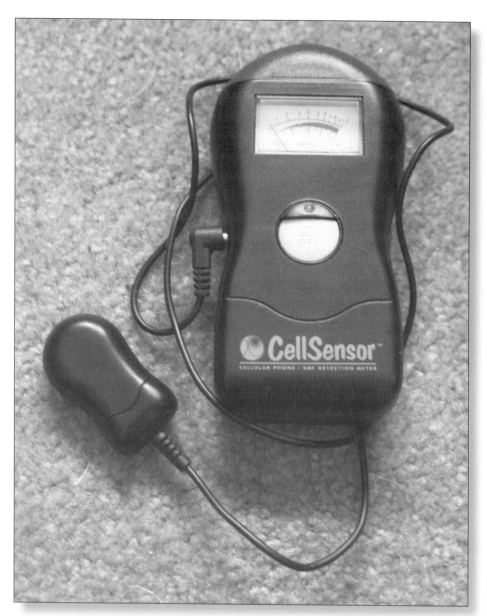

This standard EMF detector is used for measuring levels of electromagnetic energy.

might have something, but as with anything else, it is still just a best guess at this point.

Tying this device back in with Sensory Replication, if you get consistent spike activity in a particular area and that activity is dynamic, you should try to match it up with reported activity in the past. If it matches up and replicates other people's reports of the spot at the location, then you have a bit more credibility with the result. Again, the area should be thoroughly checked for alternative sources of the EMF, but it isn't likely that a breaker box or mass of wires can answer your questions regardless of how well hidden or advanced it is.

Voice Recorder

The Voice Recorder refers to personal digital recorders that record sound, usually on a flash drive, which can then be uploaded into a computer. They range in affordability and size, but they are typically fairly inexpensive and are usually smaller than most cell phones. The goal with a voice recorder is to try to catch sounds and voices that perhaps you cannot hear in the room. This can mean leaving a unit recording in a room while you are elsewhere or sleeping, or it can mean carrying it along with you on your walk-through. In addition, it can mean just recording continually while other things are going on or actively asking questions and seeing if you get a response.

What you are looking for in this scenario is what is known as Electronic Voice Phenomenon (EVP). This is basically a voice showing up in recordings or in static. There are a bunch of different devices to help with snatching voices out of static, but with a sound recorder you are just listening for voices you didn't hear at the time of your question and answer responses. Typically, the method for "question and answer" is to ask a question and wait a few moments before your next question. If it worked out, you will hear voiced responses on the playback. For the more ambient method, you just leave the device recording and listen to the playback to see if you managed any hitchhikers tagging along the audio freeway. In the very rare occasions when you catch something, it is very creepy and cool. As usual, there are caveats.

The first issue with EVP is something known as the audio Rorschach effect. This is basically the idea that when you hear sounds, your mind tries to make sense of it and will fill in the blanks to make it sound like speech or voices. Generally, this is a problem when someone posts an EVP on their website and says, "In this clip you can hear someone say, 'I'm dead, but I want a cheeseburger.'" You then listen to the clip and the vague gurgle of ambient noise starts to sound like the phrase because that is what your brain expects and fills in the blanks. If you are going to show people your EVP, you should do so by just letting the clip speak for itself. If it is super clear and everyone hears the same thing *without* being told what to hear, then you might have something, but that is based on the assumption that you are trustworthy — and that leads us to the second confound.

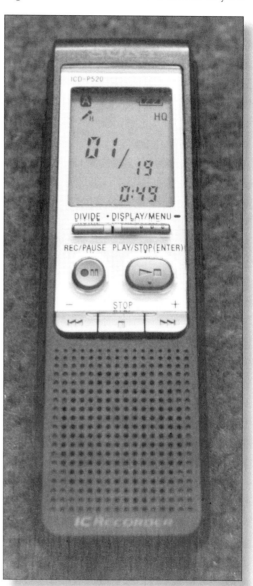

It is REALLY easy to fake audio playback. Anyone with a computer can do it with a fair amount of ease. You don't need to be part of the ILM team to add some voices into an audio track. Just get your hands on Sony ACID or Adobe Audition and you can put clips from "Star Wars" into your investigation and claim that Obi-Wan was telling you to go to Dagobah.

With this being the case, it is pretty much impossible to prove anything to anyone at all using the electronic voice phenomena. If someone does not trust you, then you are sunk. If you show up with a new speech from Abraham Lincoln

The digital voice recorder is used for capturing anomalous audio and electronic voice phenomena.

over the top of your voice recording of your White House tour, then you should expect to have your capture scrutinized like the Shroud of Turin.

Basically, what an EVP is good for in an investigation is your own personal edification and maybe a point in the direction of activity. If you get an EVP on your equipment and you know you haven't tampered with it and you know you aren't just filling in blanks, then you know to go and check out that spot again and that you have found something cool. You will be hard-pressed to convince anyone with even an ounce of skepticism of its authenticity however, and it is not going to be the lynch pin in your "Ghosts Are Real" appeal to James Randi's Million Dollar Challenge.

Digital Camera

It is always good to take a camera with you when you investigate in the off chance that you are witness to a three-ring circus of activity in front of you. We prefer digital cameras not only for the lower expense and ease of use, but also because there are fewer things that can go wrong from the click of the button to image resolution.

There is nothing technically wrong with film, but we find that the fewest number of steps is the best way. Also, unless you are doing your own developing from home, digital is the only way to keep the chain of evidence unbroken. Any number of things can happen to film from the time it leaves your hands and goes into the envelope for processing, and in all deference to photo processing professionals, you never know who is handling your material. We've all seen "Scooby-Doo" and you never know when Mr. Withers is going to sneak into the photo booth and monkey around with your photos or, if conspiracy theories involving vindictive service professionals are not your thing, then just consider that mistakes can be made that can taint and compromise your results.

Digital cameras are also usually fairly inexpensive to purchase and keep a decently low profile in your satchel or pocket. Also, no one is going to look at you funny for walking around with a camera unless you have traipsed into a secure facility or locker room, and if you are doing that, you are breaking the *no trespassing* rule anyway. Cameras are exceedingly commonplace nowadays so no one will think anything of you carrying one around to snap a few pictures. Generally you want as high a pixel resolution as you can get so we recommend that you avoid using the camera on your cell phone.

In addition to still photography, obviously you may choose to use some manner of video camera. Again, digital is the best way to go for the ease of use factor. Plugging a USB cable into a laptop is much easier than messing around with a TV's AV input or trying to sort out one of the VCR tape adapters. It should not need to be mentioned, but we are going to mention it anyway, that when walking along with your camera you should make sure you are not so focused on the taping that you walk off a ledge, down a flight of stairs, or into an end table with a priceless family heirloom, like maybe grandpa's ashes.

The reasons behind using these cameras are fairly self-explanatory, but there is more to consider than just capturing an orb or apparition. When you are doing a walk-through, it is sometimes easier to narrate your walk-through to a camera than it is to stop and write your impressions down. It gives you a more real-time feel for the events and you don't have to fumble around with materials. Also, when trying to write your results down after the fact, say in a blog entry or some kind of wrap up document for your investigation,

Any digital camera may be used for paranormal investigating.

all of it is preserved nicely on film. It also kind of helps if you see a ghost run out and dance a jig in front of you if you have a camera there ready to go.

However, there are also a couple of drawbacks to doing an audio/visual walk-through. The number one issue is that if your group is running a close walk-through, meaning the next person walking through is in the next room over, anything that he or she may hear coming from you could conceivably taint their results. If you are going to use this approach, make sure that no one can hear you do it. Either conduct your walk-through far away from the others or make it mandatory that only one person goes through at any given time.

The number two issue of this investigation method is that if you are focusing on A/V equipment you may not be paying attention to your own impressions. Sometimes people get so caught up with what is going on with their tools that they just ignore all of their feelings, which is often where the meat of the experience is to begin with. It is awesome when you get something cool on camera, but it is far rarer and generally less substantive than your own feelings and impressions.

Okay, so you may have just done a double-take at the above outlandish statement and are wondering how in the world someone's namby-pamby feelings can be more substantive than cold, hard evidence? It all goes back to the issue of fakery. Sure, someone can always lie when discussing their feelings about a situation or what they are experiencing, but the built-in checks and balances that exist in Sensory Replication excludes experiences and impressions that do not match with previously reported phenomena, so all things being equal an uninformed impression can carry much more weight than a photo that could potentially be more doctored than an extra on "Scrubs."

This brings us to orbs, which present as white circles, not unlike bubbles, that appear in photos. Sometimes you will see what looks like streaks or funnels appearing in pictures as well, which are also types of this "activity." Orbs are hotly debated in the paranormal community and there is a large movement to write them off full stop as nothing more than dust or reflections of light — and that movement has gained considerable traction in a relatively short amount of time.

We do not fully support that movement nor do we fully endorse orbs. In a profound feat of fence sitting, we hold that most of the time orbs are dust or reflections, but we're also open to the possibility that some orbs are genuine. In order to differentiate between those two possible sources, we use the same test for orbs that we would for EMF readings. If you ask the orb to move around and it follows your directions, you have something. Dust and reflections typically do not follow instructions.

~~~~~

Those are the basic pieces of equipment that we use. There are many other pieces available, but, again, they are either unproven in their effectiveness or entirely too bulky or cumbersome to make carrying them around actually feasible. Also, these are inexpensive enough to fit into most budgets and are easy enough to acquire.

Well, now that we have gone over what to do, you may find yourself asking, "What are we looking to accomplish with all this?" We've established that you're not going to be publishing any scientific papers with your results, so some people are confused as to what the mission statement of the ghost hunter is if it is not to explicitly prove the existence of ghosts and the related paranormal phenomena. The answer to that tends to vary by individual group or member.

In our specific case, we are looking to help people who are scared and worried about being crazy. Other people look to just gather cool videos, pictures, and sound clips for their own personal edification. Still others do it just to get that rush from the inherent creepiness and have a few scares. There are also those who are doing it to disprove or debunk claims of paranormal activity. All of these are valid reasons to investigate. When you get into things like greed, a desire to harm or disrupt, and generally cause mayhem, you are outside the sphere of reasonability and should look into a more constructive hobby. Of course, if your tendencies lean that way, you will be able to take up license plate-making in fairly short order anyway.

Given the above, the presentation of results varies. If you are out to kind of show off your results, then a blog or YouTube video is peachy. Of course, you have to be careful with this sort of public display because if you are doing this as a casual study you cannot be offended when skeptics show up to pull the rug out from under you. You are going to get detractors and people who will call you an idiot and will most likely drop more profanity than a Scorsese film. It helps in these cases to have the tightest results you can. If you have a grainy video in which a blob darts across the screen (is it a shadow? A flash of light? The lens cap?), then it is probably in the best interest of you and your mother's virtue that you don't post it online.

The video should also be interesting. There is nothing worse than watching a video in which the narrator drones on tonelessly about something that should be interesting, but would make a speed addict fall into a Rip Van Winkle-style coma. The paranormal is generally exciting and it takes almost special effort to make it boring. Just think about what you would want to see from a video and try to do that. Hopefully that doesn't include a painfully dry account of a Big Foot sighting so boring that we would rather watch a video on 101 ways to dry acrylic paint.

Most ghost groups have a website for their results and the stories of their exploits. This is a fine way to display results and provide your group's information to those who might be in need of an investigation. Facebook and Myspace are also great networking tools for the aspiring ghost hunter. It can be a great way to meet other like-minded individuals and share results and best practices. Sometimes it gets lonely out there in the dark and it is nice to know that you aren't the only one out there.

As with anything, it is a good idea to be careful what you put on a website and who you befriend in the field. If your website looks like it was designed by Mrs. Anderson's third grade Geography class, then it is probably going to do more harm than good. Likewise, if you befriend groups or individuals who are off their rockers or disreputable, then you are going to end up with their taint all over you. In this field, reputation is everything.

With your website, try to be as clear and make it as easy to use as possible. No one wants to see a site that looks like a kaleidoscope of words and pictures with no clear indication of what links take you where or where your eye should even fall to make heads or tails of what you are reading. There are some websites that are so convoluted that they make our eyes bleed. Trying to actually locate content should not be a chore and, if it takes people too long to find something of value, they will move on to the next item on Google.

Much like the video making, website content should be as engaging as possible. No one wants to hear about how you don't normally walk on snow because you are from a tropical island. Keep it relevant and interesting. Sure, you want to add some spice to it so it is not just a dry retelling of events, but not all flavors are equal. Tangents can be perfectly acceptable if they are entertaining and not too distracting from the main point. Again, think of what you would want to read and try to do that.

Regarding the connections that you make with other groups, it is best to find people who are generally like-minded and share your same basic attitudes, but who may also have different skills and goals in mind. That avoids messy crossover of intentions and skirts potential donnybrooks with said groups or individuals. It is always good to avoid stepping on toes where possible. This rule of thumb also lends itself to what we affectionately refer to as the "Mobius Strip of Glommage," which is a symbiotic relationship network between groups and individuals wherein they all help each other get ahead in their various ventures. It is for this reason, as well as for safety considerations, that you should screen potential glommage partners for "the crazies" or other such ailments.

Obviously someone who is not in keeping with your definition of mental stability is not a good candidate for partnership. Likewise, keep your eyes open for people who want the glommage aspect, but not the contribution. There are plenty of people out there whose first response upon hearing of a new plan or contribution is, "I want a piece of that," and have nothing at all to offer. These kinds of people are almost epidemic in frequency and never contribute in a meaningful way, but may actually hinder forward progress through hollow promises and ineffective task management. If someone is trying to hop on your gravy train, they had better be contributing to the broth or bringing along some potatoes.

Aside from the above, you also have to consider that when you align yourself with an individual or a group, you are in effect vouching for them and tying your reputation to them. If they do something ridiculous or shady, it may cause problems for you down the road. For this reason, it is good to build a relationship slowly to make sure they are the kind of people with whom you would like to be associated. It certainly bears repeating that there are a lot of people in the paranormal community who want us all to just get along and that is a good thing. It is in the best interest of no one to have some kind of West Side Story-style brawl in the streets with other gangs of investigators. It is bad form and all that snapping really monkeys with the audio gathering.

However, that being said, not everyone is on the same level out there and there are those people who are morally and ethically bankrupt. Just calling themselves investigators does not bestow some sort of magical credibility or trustworthiness upon them. There should be at least a rudimentary level of scrutiny of potential friends and allies, and if a group is going around making us all look like crazy people, then they should not just be accepted into the fold. It is a fine line we walk between being elitist jerks and responsible investigators, but it is an important line to learn and tread along carefully. When someone comes out doing shady or fraudulent things, it hurts all of us in the field. Remember that in whatever you do and you will find it easy to be a proper ambassador.

You may ask yourself what good credibility does for you if your results are not scientific enough to prove anything. That is a fair question and one many groups ask themselves over time. It is a question even more groups need to begin asking themselves as many continue to turn in evidence more dubious than that of the Holocaust deniers. The answer ties back in with the motivations of ghost hunters. If you are just trying to have a good time with your friends, then we suppose that credibility doesn't mean much outside of your circle. If you don't care about wasting your time to come up with nonsense just so you can have a laugh, then that is peachy, but if your mission statement includes anything more noble or enterprising than that, then you should probably continue to maintain credibility.

In addition to trying to help people come to terms with what is happening in their homes and letting them know they are not crazy (or that they are very much crazy, as the case may be), we have an additional agenda with our research. Given that most places with paranormal activity are the kinds of places that have been around long enough to have paranormal activity, they are very often historic locations. Obviously in the United States we don't have the same level of historic sites that England or other such countries have because our buildings are relatively young. There are those who use that fact to attempt to bulldoze their way into a more modern city and have been doing so for quite some time. Therefore, it behooves those of us who would like to preserve our historic buildings for future generations to enjoy to do whatever we can to preserve them. To that end, we have found that alleged paranormal activity is often very helpful in building up the history and mystique of a location, which then makes it more valuable a prospect and thus much more difficult to demolish in favor of another ice cream or gelato shop.

At the end of the day, everyone does this for his or her own reasons. There is no wrong answer unless that answer includes the harming or bilking of others. There is room enough in this field for anyone who wants to join so long as they comport themselves with honesty and respect and are not trying to do damage to anyone. If you can be helpful to the overall cause, then all the better.

There is no one way to go about it all, either. We have given you the guidelines we follow if you wish to adopt them. These are our best practices, which may help you in finding the method that fits your style. If you come across people who claim to have the line on the one and only true way to investigate, then understand that those people are pushing a particular agenda and are at least partially closed-minded and uninformed. If someone tells you that in order to investigate you must turn off the lights or run around in a black-painted van with the kind of equipment jammed in the back that you would find in an ITT Tech classroom, then just know that they are being a little silly and a little full of themselves. As mentioned, we have given you our best practices and it is up to you to decide what to do with them. In the following sections, there are examples of what we have chosen to do with them in pursuit of our own edification, fun, and desire for historic preservation. We leave your goals up to you.

Chapter Two:

Are Ghosts Real?

We think so… Nay, we are certain of it. Can we prove that? No, of course not. Currently, there is absolutely no definitive, indisputable proof of the existence of ghosts. The reason for the abundance of paranormal research groups is the constant pursuit of the single piece of evidence that will, once and for all, cease any arguments on the subject. We are *not* one of those groups. Since we are convinced of the existence of ghosts, we don't feel any particular compunction about not providing volumes of statistical documentation to validate our research. We know what we know, and we want to share our findings with you. We want you to decide for yourself if ghosts exist or, better yet, avail yourself to the opportunity to have your own ghostly experiences.

Can you get rid of a ghost? Let us reiterate… There is *no* irrefutable proof that ghosts exist, so there is no way to rid yourself of something whose existence cannot be proven. Many groups claim to be able to "cleanse" houses of anything from negative entities to demonic spirits. Some groups even have fancy, black box devices that purportedly emit frequencies that prevent ghosts from materializing. While it is possible, using various faith-based or meditative approaches, to redirect your mind-set so that you will no longer notice or be affected by the activity, there are no guarantees that you will be rid of your ghost.

Besides there being no way to support a claim that a house is now "clean," the very idea introduces an entire category of ethical dilemmas. If (and this is a very big "IF") you could cleanse a house of a spirit, does that mean you should? If we cannot definitively state the exact parameters of the afterlife, how do we know we aren't damning a soul to some purgatory-like existence by our flippant use of pseudo-prayer and incantation? Does the darn ghost even *want* to cross over? You get the idea. The best advice is to appreciate paranormal activity as a co-mingling of the past and present, and look to preserve this history in the same way we are looking to preserve all other history.

Types of Hauntings

As with anything involving the paranormal, at this stage of the game, there is nothing hard and fast and there is no definitive answer. However, based on years and years of research by people who are very serious about this kind of research, there has emerged a general classification for types of activity. We have discussed these classifications in detail in our previous books, but, in the spirit of completeness, we want to make sure that our new readers are sufficiently brought up to speed. These classifications are what we call the Big Three; specifically the *apparition*, *residual haunting* (place memory), and *poltergeist*.

The Apparition

Also known in some circles as an intelligent haunting, the apparition is what people typically think of when they think of a ghost. It is the literal spirit of a dead person. These entities tend to present as a shadow or a silhouette, usually either black or white in color, and are usually seen out of the corner of a person's eye.

The apparition can also look like a mist, which we believe may have contributed to the kind of cliché that puts ghosts in white sheets flittering about (and maybe chasing Pac-man). The apparition tends to display some manner of cognitive retention and appears to go about with some kind of determination. Apparitions can sometimes attempt to communicate, be it verbally, through writing of some kind, or manipulation of objects and technology, and seem to understand on some level when spoken to. If you are doing a walk-through and you are asking your EMF to spike a specific pattern or number of times and it capitulates, you are dealing with an apparition.

An important thing to note about apparitions: While they are vaguely human-shaped, they do not tend to bear the features of a specific person, nor do they present with clothing or objects. This is because they are spirits (if you are a religious person) and energy (if you are not), but either way, a pair of overalls doesn't have the wherewithal to hang out with a person after physical death. Not only can you not take them along, you can't even borrow them. If you are pausing to wonder what about your Uncle Zeke's story about seeing a full-frontal, see-through Obi-Wan complete with a steering wheel from a '57 Chevy in one hand and a bottle of Jack Daniels in the other, you will be delighted to find that you've segued us right into the next classification.

Residual Haunting

The residual haunting can be confusing for people. Given that the term "haunting" is used to describe a location with activity as well as describing the act itself, many people find themselves a bit turned around. That the residual haunting turns out not to be a real ghost or spirit does little to make the public at-large less flummoxed, though truthfully, the public at-large most likely is not even aware that this classification exists. The residual haunting is a repetitive and recurring event that plays out the same way time and time again. It is believed to be a recording on space and time that repeats on a loop...much like a videotape.

The general idea is that whatever event is being depicted had so much emotional resonance it was forever captured for posterity. The hows and whys of this are anyone's guess, but there are theories from the memory of molecules (the body exchanges all its old molecules for new ones every seven years, but manages to retain preferences, physical details, and memories) to some forms of rock having the potential to record events (limestone, for one). Even still, no one knows for sure why this happens.

The way it typically plays out is that a person will see a fully dressed, full-featured person going about some action or another complete with accessories. This usually happens at regular intervals, be it every night or on the same night every year or some other schedule, and is always exactly the same. There is no intelligence here and it is impossible to interact with this event. Sometimes more than one figure can be present like the old tried and true "little girl being chased by the mean man with a beard" (or any combination of experiences involving the oft-reported ghost of a little girl or an old man), but it can just as easily be only one figure or even just an object.

These can be very dramatic and scary, but you should always bear in mind that this cannot hurt you or affect you in any way. If you see a Paul Bunyan look-alike bearing down on you with a chainsaw, then it is probably just a residual haunting — or it's a Paul Bunyan look-alike trying to have at you with a chainsaw. As always, we leave it to you to discern, as you have to take it on a case-by-case basis.

The Poltergeist

This is the big one — the one that everyone wants to hear about because it is very dramatic and visually appealing. It is the one where things fly around the room and fall to the floor violently. Granted, if the objects in question are a delicate Mayan wood carving you bought for two grand at the import store and the urn containing Grandma Edna, it might not be so cool. Much like the residual haunting, the poltergeist is mistakenly called a ghost or spirit when the general consensus amongst professionals is that this is not a ghost at all. What it is believed to be requires a bit of explanation.

Most people are familiar with the concept of telekinesis in some way. The term is out-dated and is now called psychokinesis or PK, but it refers to the ability to manipulate objects with a person's mind. PK can be on a macro level, like spoon bending or moving objects, to micro level like psychic surgery or the manipulation of objects on a molecular level. We are not going to argue the relative merits of claims of such abilities here as it is not at all the point of this book and it is only being explained insofar as it relates to poltergeists. However, there are many magicians and sleight of hand artists who specialize in showing how spoon bending in particular can be faked. Having done spoon bending myself, I can speak to the fact that just because it can be faked using sleight of hand does not mean that it cannot be legitimately performed. It is a general misconception of how spoon bending operates that leads such debunkers to believe they have proven and exposed the chicanery of "evil paranormal investigators." Remember, a heart attack can be faked, but that does not disprove the existence of heart attacks.

Poltergeist activity is believed to be the result of an unconscious lashing out by a human agent with PK energy, which results in the movement of objects. This human agent can be of either sex, although you tend to hear about women most often. There is generally some source of stress in the person's life and is most commonly associated with hormonal changes like puberty. Because of how high profile and dynamic these kinds of events can be, poltergeist activity has come under scrutiny and is often under fire by skeptics. Like anything else with the paranormal, the general inability to replicate in a lab setting is a major downfall. Poltergeist activity goes one better and becomes difficult to replicate in the home itself. People reason that since it is a person doing it, ultimately they must have control of it and can do it at will. Such hard-core pressure has led to some subjects picking something up and throwing it just to make the researcher go away.

This idea that someone should be able to control something just because they are generating it is really tiresome and unfair. It is much like someone suffering from a somatoform disorder — a disorder that has no medical basis at all, but is generated entirely from a person's head. An example of this would be Glove Paralysis, which causes a person's hands from the wrist up to be completely paralyzed and without feeling. The way your nerves and tendons work make it physically impossible for such a problem to occur, so the paralysis is entirely mental on the patient's part. Where people run into trouble is when they say that such a disorder isn't real and is "all in your head" as if knowing there is no physical cause that will make it go away. Only through therapy and, in some cases, drug treatments can the disorder be overcome. Poltergeist activity works the same way. Just because a person is doing it subconsciously, they cannot just start or stop making things fly around the room at will. It is generally only after the stress the person is under is relieved and the overreaching issues solved that the activity will cease.

~~~~~

Those are the Big Three and, while they are far and away the most common types of activity investigators encounter, they're not the only games in town. One notable type of activity is the *crisis apparition*, a well-known and well-reported event in which a person sees a loved one appear out of nowhere, often when said loved one is hundreds of miles away. The loved one will usually wave or say something like, "I love you," or "Goodbye." The viewer then calls to check on the loved one only to find out that the loved one has just died unexpectedly and often at the same time they appeared to the viewer. There is some amount of support for this phenomenon in people who report back from *near death experiences* (NDE). Many people who have an NDE report seeing a guide who allows them to visit their relatives one last time only to wake after being resuscitated or, in one reported case, right before the coroner made his first Y incision.

Occasionally, you will hear of a living person presenting in this way to a loved one, usually when the person is in great peril. There is a fairly famous story regarding a man with a broken leg lost in the wilderness appearing to friends and family to bring help. Coma patients can also get into the action, but this tends to lead into another form of activity. The *out of body experience* (OBE) is a fairly common encounter or event when performing paranormal investigations.

Also referred to as astral projection, this is essentially when a person's "spirit" leaves his or her body and goes for a stroll around the ethereal plane. The modality of a person's locomotion during this kind of excursion differs from person to person and can range from flying to walking. Some people report seeing a golden or silver cord attached to them, which they believe keeps them connected to their physical body. This is determined completely by a person's expectations and reports of these cords being severed leading to a lost soul wandering the Earth have been greatly exaggerated or woven from whole cloth. This is a phenomenon that is hard to swallow for some people, but it is reported with a frequency that would make us remiss if we failed to include it. That we have had our own experiences with it makes it all the more crucial for inclusion.

So there we have the major players in the game. The variety of activity and particular details of each can make things a little confusing, especially when you are sifting through evidence trying to hash out just what the heck is going on. One thing we think makes it helpful but could potentially pile on the frustration is that none of these things are mutually exclusive. If you have a lamp floating across the room while a mist is hovering in the corner by the entertainment center and a dude in a mechanics jacket looks like he is going to jack you with a pipe wrench, it is not just some kind of a big Super Ghost, but rather a bunch of things happening simultaneously. The stress from an apparition or residual haunting can bring on poltergeist activity and maybe the event that created the apparition left an impression on time and space, which then proceeds to appear to chase you down the hallway as if you were in A-ha's Take on Me video.

Joining a Group

Although this tutorial is aimed at individuals or small groups of individuals wanting to get their feet wet in the sea of ghost-hunting, we totally understand that some people would prefer to join a larger group because there is both safety and anonymity in larger numbers. No matter where you live or what motivates your desire for paranormal investigation, there are numerous groups across the country that could be a good fit for your paranormal investigating style. However, there are also numerous groups across the country that might be crazy and want to investigate the paranormal activity in your wallet or inside your blouse. We have recently heard reports of paranormal group meetings that involved generous servings of alcohol and a mix-and-match approach to "clothing optional" pairings of a decidedly questionable nature…and this was a group that was SUPPOSEDLY well-respected (although, in all honesty, they were the only game in town during their heyday). The point being is this: If you are looking to join a paranormal investigation group, do your homework and research them. With the abundance of groups available and actively looking for members, it is okay to interview them much in the same way you might interview potential schools for your children. Don't be hasty. If you invest the time to be selective with your paranormal alliance, you will reap a much greater reward in terms of learning the ropes and you might even make some great friends in the process.

So, how do you spot a bad ghost-hunting group? We are going to get down to the nitty-gritty of what to avoid when aligning yourself with any one particular group. Keep in mind that there are many variations on what constitutes an acceptable investigation, but there are just as many investigative groups that are nothing but loose cannons, more concerned about generating revenue than observing accepted methodologies.

"Red Flags"

The following is the meat and potatoes of it. While there are numerous other idiosyncratic behaviors that might be suggestive of a group whose members may be slightly off their collective "nut," as long as they adhere — for the most part — to these basic guidelines, you can enjoy a sense of guarded comfort in knowing that the investigating team you have selected will probably not turn out to be the next Heaven's Gate cult.

Membership Fees: Membership is contingent upon payment, with higher membership fees getting you greater access. Now, this is America, and free enterprise reigns supreme. There is nothing illegal about charging membership fees to belong to any group, including paranormal investigation. The question that you have to ask is this: What am I getting in return for my membership fee? If you are regularly tithing to a group or an organization that rarely schedules investigations or workshops, where is that money going? It is entirely up to the readers to decide if a pay-for-play approach matches their agenda, but we believe that there are just as many good ghost hunting groups that don't charge for membership.

Equipment: Their website indicates use of non-standard and "custom" equipment. In order to achieve results that have any validity at all, it is important to use equipment that is recognized as "standard" by the ghost-hunting community. Without going into an exhaustive list of every possible piece of equipment, a good rule of thumb is this: Does the piece of equipment serve a purpose outside of ghost hunting? Since most pieces of equipment generally used on an investigation were devices that already existed and were co-opted into paranormal investigating, if you don't recognize it or it is something created by the group for a use that cannot be measured or documented (think, "We invented this device that you can plug into your wall and it will keep ghosts from materializing!"), then it likely is just an attention-seeking ploy from a less-than-honest organization. You are best served by bringing your particular skill set to another group's table.

Organization: It is nearly impossible to pull off a successful investigation without having an extremely well-run organization. Reputable groups have specific routines and protocols that are followed when organizing and implementing an investigation, often delegating specific tasks to certain members for each portion of the process. This is important for two reasons. First, it allows all data and evidence to be collected in a tidy, methodical fashion. Disorganization can taint evidence and completely disrupt even the most well-intentioned investigation. Second, disorganized groups that lack proper protocol often make it difficult for other groups to get a foothold on a given community. More than a few times, we have encountered locations that were unwilling to participate or be even remotely cooperative with our research based on their past experiences with groups that talked a good game, but completely screwed the pooch during the actual investigation.

Appearance: This is the third book we have written, and we cannot stress this point enough. Please, we beseech you: resist the temptation to don combat boots and fatigues. Berets are OUT OF THE QUESTION! We will concede the occasional trench coat or fedora, when used exclusively of each other and only in context with current fashion, but cloaks are totally unacceptable, unless you are investigating the Renaissance Festival. Our goal is to help legitimize the entire process of paranormal investigation, so it's particularly disconcerting when groups with a flair for the dramatic favor role-playing over research. Let's try likening it to a crime scene investigation. How do you think you would feel as the victim of a crime if some joker dressed like Sherlock Holmes showed up, basset hound in tow, to take your statement and search for clues with his gigantic magnifying glass? I am guessing your reaction might be akin to, "Dude, are you friggin' kidding me?" The same decorum shown in any other profession outside of miming and freak shows should be utilized when implementing a paranormal investigation. People who already think they are crazy needn't have the notion exacerbated by the arrival of the Society for Creative Anachronism ceremoniously caravanning up to your house in a modified ice cream truck. Also, be advised — wearing chain mail will almost certainly get you a good, solid ass-kicking.

Methodology: If they have adopted their "methodology" from the television, well, I'm just going to break it down, right now: There is currently NO televised ghost show using any scientifically established and controlled protocol to investigate. These shows are for entertainment purposes only and, honestly, should be advertised as such. If you find that a potential group mimics what they saw last Wednesday on "Dish Network," look elsewhere. Again, while there is no harm in playing ghost hunter with a few of your friends (providing you are not engaging in any activity that is potentially harmful or illegal), if the group you have contacted advertises itself as a "scientific" group, it isn't. It's that simple.

Chapter Three:

Mark Boccuzzi and EVPs

Paranormal investigating has come a long way from the days of a lens flare being considered a "good capture," and, while the current trend has not necessarily moved away from photo and video evidence, it has definitely turned its attention to the direction of Electronic Voice Phenomena or EVP. Collecting EVP is a process in which investigators use a number of different methods to capture voices believed to be those of deceased persons. Often, voices can be heard upon playback that were not audible at the time of the recording. Interest in this area of investigating has recently piqued, and what once could only be studied with a handheld recorder is now achievable with a number of new devices that have been created or modified just for this purpose with very compelling results.

Since we have only limited experience with the vast and varied devices or protocols for the collection of EVP, we decided that we would seek out an expert on the topic and find out a little more information. We recently sat down with our good friend, Mark Boccuzzi, a research scientist at Windbridge Institute for Applied Research in Human Potential. Mark, who is considered an expert in the field, had this to say:

Q: What, in your words, is EVP?
A: Traditionally, electronic voice phenomena (EVP) is said to occur when voices — the source of which has no conventional explanation — are captured on audio recordings. With new developments in technology, the definition of EVP has been

expanded to include intelligible speech that is electronically generated by devices or software allegedly affected by an unidentified influence.

Q: Tell us about the following devices: Frank's Box, Paranormal Puck, Radio Shack Hack, EVP Maker, Ovilus. How do they work?

A: Obviously, there is a lot to say about this, and I could easily fill a book with information about these devices, how they work, their underlying theories, and their effectiveness, but since I have limited space, this will be very general.

These devices represent the latest trend in EVP collection. While they all allegedly produce paranormal voices, they actually utilize several very different methods, which include radio sweep, random selection, and environmental monitoring. Each of these is discussed in turn below. However, before we talk about these newer methods, let's take a moment and review what I like to call "traditional EVP" or the "voice on tape" phenomena.

Originally, recording for EVP was not conducted exclusively at haunted locations. In fact, the majority of the early EVP work was conducted in labs or in people's homes. It wasn't until much later that it became a tool used by ghost hunters. Even today, people use EVP recording as a method of spirit communication to connect with departed loved ones or even to get advice from spirit guides or other entities.

In the early days of EVP research, the equipment was very simple. Sarah Estep, researcher and founder of the American Association of Electronic Voice Phenomena (now Association TransCommunication), wrote in her book *Voices of Eternity* that her original equipment was "limited to an old tape recorder, a microphone that whistled at inconvenient times, and headphones in which the right earpiece was dead."

The process used to capture these voices on tape was not very complicated. One simply set up a tape recorder, added some type of background sound (like running water, an electric fan, or a white noise generator), started recording, and began asking questions. When done, the tape was played back (listening with headphones to hear all the details in the recording) and any voices that might have been captured were noted.

While the equipment and methods were simple, it took perseverance before results were achieved. Researchers set up a dedicated space for their equipment and attempted communication each day at a specific time. It has been reported that it sometimes took several weeks before they actually started to record voices. As recording technology advanced, cassette recorders replaced the old reel-to-reel tape recorders and those have now been replaced with digital recorders. However, while the technology has changed, the basic method has remained the same. That is, until now.

Radio Sweep

The radio sweep method of recording for EVP is simple and requires an audio recorder and a standard AM/FM radio (like your clock radio). To record radio sweep, start the audio recorder, turn on the radio, and start turning the tuning knob up the dial. When the knob gets to the end of the dial, change direction and go back down. By repeating this process you are "sweeping" up and down the radio band, hearing short snippets of voices, music, static, etc. The speed at which you sweep the dial is up to you. Now, as you continue to sweep the radio, start asking questions out loud — about one question every ten to fifteen seconds. After about a minute, stop sweeping, turn off the audio recorder and the radio, and play back your recording. By using this method, some people claim that they hear relevant responses to their questions in the radio noise when they listen to the recording.

One thing that is important to note here is that unlike traditional EVP where you need to play the recording back in order to hear any captured voices, the radio sweep method allows you to hear the audio stream as it is being produced. This means that if you are listening carefully, you might be able to hear responses to your questions thus allowing for you to hold an actual real-time conversation. This idea of communication in real-time has become a trend in the development of new EVP technologies.

Frank's Box and the MiniBox are devices that automate the radio sweep process. These devices contain a radio receiver and other electronics that automatically sweep up and down the AM or FM radio band. Some versions have controls that allow you to set the speed of the sweep, the range (how far up or down the band they sweep), and the sensitivity of the receiver. It is my understanding that Frank Sumption no longer builds or sells his box, but the MiniBox is [at the time of this writing] available for sale on-line. Depending on the model, prices generally range from $300 to $600.

The Radio Shack Hack is a modified Radio Shack AM/FM portable radio. The "hack" was developed as an easy way to build an inexpensive alternative to Frank's Box. Detailed directions for how to make the modification can be found on-line, but the general idea is that the mute pin of the radio is cut, which causes the receiver to automatically and continually sweep the radio band. In the hacked radios I have seen, the rate of the sweep is not adjustable.

Opinions about the effectiveness of these devices, and the radio sweep method in general, vary greatly. Some operators are convinced that they can use these devices to make contact with different non-corporeal entities while some critics believe that any alleged communication is simply the misinterpretation of the fragmented radio sounds by over-enthusiastic operators.

Random Selection

Systems based on the random selection method to capture EVP typically use a random or pseudorandom routine to make a selection from a library of sounds. Once selected, the sound is then played. EVPMaker software by Stefan Bion, for example, cuts up an audio file into small segments, which then become the library of sounds. When an operator starts an EVP recording session, the software randomly picks a segment and plays it back. The program allows the operator to choose from several randomization schemes including a pseudorandom number generator, accessing random number data from the Internet, or receiving random numbers from specialized random number generator hardware attached to the computer.

The EVPMaker software was created to generate background noise for traditional EVP recordings (to replace white noise or running water). For example, an operator would have an audio file of crowd sounds. This file would be put into the EVPMaker and a random stream of noise would be produced. The operator would then turn on an audio recorder and start asking questions. After the session was completed, the operator would listen to the recording to see if any EVP was captured.

Recently, people have been using the EVPMaker in a slightly different way. In May 2008, Bion posted directions on how to load a specially designed audio file into EVPMaker. This audio file contains seventy-two small units of speech known as allophones, which become the sound library for the software. Using this file, the EVPMaker can generate an audio stream of word fragments that some operators claim can be manipulated by an entity to form recognizable words and phrases. Like radio sweep, the operator can hear this audio stream during the EVP sessions, thus allowing for the possibility of real-time communication.

Environmental Monitoring

This method combines environmental sensors (like electromagnetic field meters and thermometers) with specialized software and speech generation. Examples of systems using this method include the Paranormal Puck and the Ovilus (both created by Digital Dowsing).

An early version of the Paranormal Puck, made by Digital Dowsing, LLC.

The Paranormal Puck is a small box that plugs into the USB port of a computer. The Puck is basically an environmental sensor package that contains Hall effect sensors (to measure electromagnetic fields), temperature sensors, and other components. The software that comes with the Puck contains a library of words. Once an EVP session is started, the software will monitor the environmental data coming from the Puck hardware and then, using a specific algorithm, select and play back words from its library. It is important to note that that the process used to select which word is spoken is not a random one (as is the case with the EVPMaker), but based on the amount and direction of environmental change as sensed by the hardware.

Q: Now, tell me anything that you would consider crucial when attempting to collect EVP.

A: While collecting any type of paranormal evidence, people should always keep the following guidelines in mind:

1. Remember to properly and completely document all processes and procedures. Failing to do so not only prevents others from learning about what procedures work and don't work, but also impedes the ability to refine and perfect effective methods.

2. While recording for EVP, develop and follow procedures that actively control for any and all extraneous sounds that might be misinterpreted as actual EVP.

3. When reviewing recordings, be aware of and control the perceptual biases of the reviewers (i.e., the desire to find an EVP and the mind's tendency to misinterpret noise and randomness as having order and meaning). While it may be impossible to completely rule out perceptual problems when reviewing paranormal evidence, by using carefully designed and documented procedures *(see #2!)*, you can at least demonstrate that you have controlled for non-paranormal explanations.

4. If you choose to report your findings or post your EVP recordings online, be sure to provide as much information as you can about your procedures including how the EVP was recorded, what equipment was used, etc. While posting a short audio segment with a strange sound is fun, it does not help to prove that an actual EVP was recorded nor does it help us further our understanding of the phenomenon.

The Ovilus is the only device we have had any practical experience with. We tagged along with a friend of ours who has one to a location that was believed to have a lot of paranormal activity. He fired up the Ovilus and let it do its thing. During the few minutes it was "speaking," it threw out a fair amount of significant words — and even one gunshot. We are even fairly certain we heard it say "Patrick," even though that is not listed as one of its programmed words.

While the Ovilus, which is clearly labeled *For Entertainment Purposes*," may not be the most accurate device for getting EVP, it still left us scratching our heads a little bit, trying to figure out how it was able to come up with words that were relevant to the situation. It's weird stuff.

However, now that everyone knows the proper guidelines for capturing and cataloging EVP (thank you, Mark!), you can be certain that every EVP you capture is a clean catch and certainly worthy of consideration in the argument for the existence of intelligent interaction with the discarnate soul.

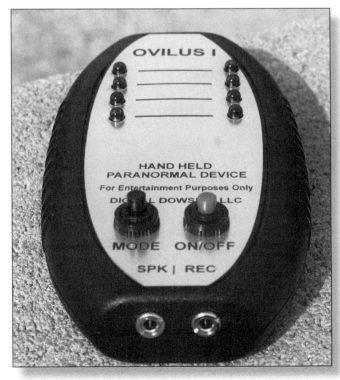

An early version of the Ovilus, made by Digital Dowsing, LLC.

Chapter Four:

Patrick Wraps it Up

I have to pause a minute and re-iterate something because in-depth discussion of this makes me feel silly without the caveat that we, Wailing Bansidhe Investigations, have no interest in proving anything to anyone nor are we interested in arguing the existence of ghosts. I have had many experiences in my life that have convinced me ghosts are real. If you don't believe in ghosts, you will find nothing here that is going to change your mind. We talk about ghosts as if they were real because we believe in them; if you don't believe in them, good for you, though I am not sure why you are reading this and not following Christopher Hitchens or James Randi around like that little dog from Looney Tunes.

This may sound insulting, but frankly I am tired of having people who seem to have the IQ and writing skill of a cow turd coming onto paranormal websites and spewing vitriolic missives about how people who believe in ghosts or the paranormal are all morons who have less than a high school education and we should be ashamed of ourselves. I am not sure exactly who crapped in these people's cereal, but I have had enough of it. I don't troll skeptics' boards telling them they are wrong at best and stupid at worst and I would appreciate the same courtesy. That being said, you will never find anyone more self-righteous than the atheist who often times is just as dogmatic and closed-minded as the most true-believer zealot. Anyone who denies even the slightest possibility of an alternate scenario in favor of intellectual elitism is an idiot. There, I said it — and I won't apologize for it.

The point of all this is to come up with results as untainted as possible. Given the criticisms so often leveled at the believer in the paranormal, it does not do anyone any good to have sloppy and faulty investigations. This is why it is important to make sure that no information is shared amongst investigators until the final phase — that phase is the wrap up/wrap down session in which you sit down with whomever it is that knows the stories and compare notes. You go through your walk-through results and see if that matches up with any reported activity in the past. If you have, you have scored a direct hit. If you have described a feeling or experience in the general area of the reported activity that matches up, it is a softer hit. Five direct hits and you've sunk your opponent's battleship — or, at the very least, you are having some fabulous success with your investigation.

As we mentioned earlier, our method is a modified Sensory Replication method. We do not go the full nine into statistics and scientific result gathering. If you want to do that, you are going to have to feed the numbers into a chi square statistical analysis and compare that against chance to see if your results are significant. For our purposes, again those being mere documentation and no-you-are-not-nutsery, we are not concerned with those things. If you are setting out to investigate on your own, you don't have to be either. If you make your business the aforementioned "trying to prove it scientifically," then you need to do this and a lot of other stuff that should include college coursework on research methods and sound science, but that just isn't our goal.

A common question we get about this process is, "How do I know what to write down on the walk-through?" There is no really easy answer for that beyond just saying you should write down everything that you feel, particularly anything out of the ordinary. I have found time and time again that the things that I think are silly or I have almost dismissed out of hand are what turn out to be the strongest hits. Of course, when you are doing the walk-through it is important to take note of your surroundings. If you are getting dizzy or light-headed, a check to make sure that there is not some kind of natural gas leak going on is a good idea. Likewise, if you are experiencing a hot or cold feeling, check to make sure you aren't standing under the A/C vent or next to a radiator or operating stove.

Not to belabor the point, but generally people expect lots of excitement when they do investigations. They have seen the movies and TV shows and they expect to be slimed or drowned by statues that have sprung to life. This is not generally the case. I cannot speak for everyone, but I would be very surprised to hear a credible account of any of that kind of nonsense. Usually the activity is smaller, and if you ignore those small impressions, you will miss a lot of good results.

Another misconception people have about investigating is that you have to be born with some innate sensitivity to the paranormal to be a successful investigator. Every paranormal show parades psychics and mediums out as if they are the be-all-end-all authority on all things paranormal. This is just not the case. I am not saying that all psychics and mediums are frauds, but anyone can investigate haunted places and have experiences. It is a skill like any other that gets better with practice and can be cultivated. It is true that some people have a greater predisposition to this than others, but that doesn't mean that they are the only ones who can do it.

Of course, at the end of the day, it doesn't do you much good to know how to look if you don't know what you are looking for. We've talked about writing down feelings and experiences you have, but those by themselves are just a collection of data or pieces of a puzzle. It helps to know what the picture is supposed to look like when you are done. Now, do not make the mistake that we are advocating the shoehorning of data. Shoehorning is a confound that discredits many investigators as they show up trying to make the evidence fit their preconceived notion of what is going on rather than letting the evidence build to a cohesive and rational conclusion. Many skeptics call foul on this particular play as the over-zealous investigator can take otherwise explainable events and make them into proof positive of their premise.

Alliteration aside, this is very bad. The skeptics don't need any more help from the investigators to claim that we are all a bunch of uneducated charlatans out to bilk the working class of their hard-earned dollars whilst they themselves sit in ivory towers of rationalism drinking the drink of the superior. The skeptic loves nothing more than to punch holes in your experiences despite the fact that they know very little about what it is we do. So the answer to this is to be as tight as possible. It will not be good enough for them, but then nothing ever really is. Always be aware of Occam's razor, which says the simplest of explanations is often the correct one. Sometimes this works out to explain your dizzy spell away as a reaction to a local perfume or generalized dementia, and sometimes the more skeptical answer reads as realistic as Scully trying to explain to Mulder how she still doesn't believe in aliens even after roughly fourteen rides in their spaceship and various associated shenanigans. Sometimes it is more plausible to just go with the ghosts.

When we say that you should know what the picture is supposed to look like, we mean that you should know what your collection of evidence should equal if you have ruled out the more mundane causes. Oftentimes people believe that all activity stems from the same thing; those nebulous "haunting" phenomena that is sort of all-encompassing. It is generally believed not to be the case.

We have established how to investigate, what you are likely to find, and how to put the pieces together, so where do you go from here? This is a fine question and in a general sense it is up to you. As we've mentioned, we are motivated by helping people realize that perhaps they are not crazy, or the inverse and they should seek immediate psychiatric help and maybe they would be so kind as to stop choking us. We are also motivated to document on some anecdotal level the experiences that we have had in the hopes it will help other like-minded individuals find their way. You might just want to feel the thrill of the experience or you might want to study further and contribute scientifically. What you will *not* be able to do in any meaningful way is to rid people of their ghostly affliction. Since "Ghostbusters" hit the scene in 1984, people have been under the misconception that there is a way to free their homes of what they perceive as spectral vermin, as if a paranormal investigator is some kind of supernatural exterminator. While some investigators might bill themselves with this kind of ability, it is, unfortunately, a decent helping of hogwash.

While there are some investigation teams that fix leaky pipes and replace hot water heaters in their day jobs, calling said investigators in to look at your property isn't going to terminate with those investigators carrying out a smoking trap full'o'ghost to be kept in a custom-made storage facility in their basement no matter what they might claim on their website. If they show up with a bunch of custom equipment and a Jacob's Ladder claiming that it helps draw in or repel ghosts, understand that custom equipment is fairly worthless, as the results need to be carried out on standardized equipment if any result is to be taken seriously. All a Jacob's Ladder does is look cool in science fiction movies when you need something science-y in the background while some madman is raising a mishmash of body parts from the dead using lighting and a healthy dose of insanity.

Whether or not there is merit to people who claim to "cross over" spirits, which is an attempt by a medium or psychic to help the spirit leave our world and go to whatever afterlife is awaiting, it is very important that while investigations can help people understand what is going on, they should never be offered as a paid service. It is one thing to make money on ancillary endeavors relating to the paranormal, like, oh, I don't know, writing a book, but charging people for investigating and/or removing spirits is a huge no-no in the paranormal world.

The reasons to refrain from charging should be self-explanatory, but in the interest of completeness, we will lay it out. The first and most pressing issue is that when you charge for an investigation there is the expectation that certain results should be met. We doubt we are alone in the feeling that if we pay $350 for something we should get something more than, "Nope, sorry, nothing is here."

When dollar signs are introduced to the paranormal investigation scenario, the pressure is on to be worth it. Unfortunately this often translates into the fudging of data at best and outright fakery at worst. Obviously if the field is to ever be taken with anything more than a grain of salt, such behavior is beyond inappropriate.

The next issue is related to the first. Because nothing in the paranormal can be definitively proven at this point, you are essentially asking for payment for a service that is completely subjective and the risk for rampant abuse is about as high as an ATM with its money door open. It is inconceivable to a respectable and legitimate group to expect someone to pony up cash so you can tell them that maybe, just maybe Aunt Tessie might still be going about her business in your laundry room fifteen years after her death.

Another issue with charging for this kind of service is just flat creepiness. Making your money off the fear of genuinely troubled individuals is taking advantage to a ghoulish level. I am not sure how those who engage in this practice sleep at night, as it is making money off of the backs of the hurting and afraid. Such groups should be ashamed of themselves and should not be taken seriously in the field.

When you are involved in an area of study in which the things you are studying may or may not exist, charging for services should never enter into the conversation at all.

Lastly, there is no guarantee that the services offered are in any way legitimate. Even if you take the premise that the paranormal is wholly real and valid, there is no way at all to prove that crossing over methods or whatever service is being provided is in any way on the level. If you couple that with the discussion of the Big Three, you will see that only one of the classifications would benefit from a crossing-over even if such a thing were possible.

As valid of a field as we believe the paranormal to be, you should always be aware there are those out there looking to take advantage and exploit the sensitivities, religious beliefs, and superstitions of people in a weakened state. Just like anything else, being forewarned is being forearmed and you always have to be as professional and respectful as possible. Whatever your goals, making money from the investigations themselves should never be included in them. The one caveat to that would be the haunted public location that offers some sort of limited investigation-like activity around Halloween for a fee or some such thing is a slightly different matter. If you go into it knowing it is a for-entertainment venture, then the money paid becomes no different than what you might spend on a movie, concert, or play. It should be fairly clear, however, where the difference lies in this kind of scenario and an elderly couple who can't sleep at night because their closet is saying profane and threatening things to them.

~~~~~

I think by now we have pretty well drilled it into your head to approach paranormal investigation with as much caution as you have enthusiasm. Honestly, though, that can never be said enough, but, since we have all but belabored the point, it is time for the good stuff — *the ghosts*. Without further ado, let us prepare to visit a few of the best places in the greater Phoenix area to catch a glimpse of an apparition or hear a disembodied voice on playback announcing, "I'm here!" You may even be lucky enough to feel the icy touch of a hand, reaching out from the great beyond… All right, settle down. We ask that you secure your belongings and keep your arms and legs inside the ride at all times because here we go.

Section Two

Haunted Hangouts
of Phoenix

Exterior shot of Sean Larkin's childhood home... the Eisendrath House.

Chapter Five:

The Eisendrath House

When we first met Sean Larkin, we were giving a lecture and book signing in Scottsdale for *Scare-Izona*. He approached us with such enthusiasm about his childhood home that was positively exploding with paranormal activity, but knowing that we routinely like to know as little as possible about a location before we investigate, he simply left the carrot dangling before us and promised to get in touch with us in the future about the property.

True to his word, he emailed us a short while later and explained that the home he described was none other than the Eisendrath House, a very well-known historic home in the city of Tempe. Originally, the hope was that we could get inside the building for a bit of a look-see, but even though the city of Tempe, (which now owns the property), was on board with our investigation, the builder who is in charge of the impending restoration quickly kiboshed our plans…some business about it being a huge liability and being structurally unsound and completely unsafe, or some such relatively major technicality. In any event, we would have to invoke Plan B.

We met up with Sean outside the Arizona Historical Society in Tempe, which just happens to be right next-door to the house. From the road, it doesn't really lend itself to the term "mansion," even though it is sometimes referred to as such, because it does not offer the same countenance that leaps to mind when the word is bandied about. There are no big, iron gates, Gothic columns, or gargoyles. However, that certainly does not take anything away from its commanding presence and historic significance.

The Eisendrath was built in 1930 as a winter home for Rose Eisendrath, the wife of a wealthy Chicago glove maker, so that she may enjoy the mild Arizona winters without subjecting herself to the discrimination she faced from local resorts as a result of her Jewish heritage. She was residing in the home at the time of her death in 1936. It was at that point that Sean's grandparents purchased the home, which stayed in his family for many years. He lived there until he left home for school.

Tragic History

Sean led us up the gravelly hillside to the house, which now stands in marked disrepair. Being careful to avoid open septic holes, we made our way to the oddly out-of-place red brick patio. At that point, Sean asked us if we wanted to walk around on our own

The red brick patio has replaced the home's original pool in which Sean Larkin's grandmother drowned.

to see if we got a "vibe" on anything, or if we wanted to go straight for "the meaty stuff." We opted to go straight for the dish. Without missing a beat, Sean pointed to the bricked patio and said, "This was the swimming pool that's all bricked over…where my grandmother drowned." Not expecting the history to get that meaty so fast, I gasped. He explained that she was only 36-years-old when she drowned, and rumors began circulating that suggested the possibility of foul play.

We continued walking the premises, and Sean stopped us at the side of the house where he, accompanied by a childhood friend named Emily, had his most compelling run-in with the paranormal.

Pointing to the walls that correspond with particular rooms of the house, he explained what happened, "This is a dining room here, and there's a little covered pantry area. One door goes into the dining room, and one goes into the kitchen…it had some cupboards with dishes in it…I would have been about 12 or 13…Emily walked through [the door] to take some stuff to the dining room, and I was right behind her…two glasses came down in succession [from the cupboard]."

Picking up two rocks from the ground, Sean slammed them with great force into the exterior wall of the house. "Just like that… they were like 'BAM BAM!' at an angle… That was one of the more interesting things," he said.

We continued the tour around the building and back to the front of the house, which prompted Sean to relay another ghostly experience. "During Christmas time — we spent Christmas here in 1968 — I don't remember if it was Christmas Eve or Christmas morning, but we all came down and the garland had been ripped down and the tree had been upended."

While this may not stand alone as a definitive example of paranormal activity, it certainly becomes more compelling when coupled with the allegation that the home's original owner, Rose Eisendrath, died *in* the home…*on Christmas Eve*!

Sean quietly contemplates the ghostly shenanigans that took place in this home, which is currently being restored to its original splendor.

Conclusion

These tales only scratch the surface of the paranormal activity at the Eisendrath.

Sean went on to describe a few other events, including one situation where his sister was unable to fall asleep in her bedroom one evening because the sounds of a phantom "cocktail party" were keeping her awake. He also told us of a visiting family friend being startled at the sight of a ghostly couple standing at the foot of her bed. The spectral woman asked the friend how Sean's mother was doing. As it turns out, the description of the couple was exactly that of Sean's grandmother and step-grandfather.

This home is very near and dear to Sean, and it is absolutely vital that the home — as well as its rich history of paranormal goings-on — be preserved for future generations to enjoy. Currently, efforts are being made to expedite the preservation process so that the home can start its new life as the City of Tempe Water Conservation offices, as well as providing public meeting space.

Chapter Six:

The George and Dragon Pub

Katie's Investigation Notes

Honestly, I'm not a barfly. I blend into a bar crowd about as seamlessly as Napoleon would into the NBA. I stand out like a sore thumb. However, if you throw a ghost or two into the mix, I will gladly let my arm be twisted. Such was the case with the George and Dragon Pub. Since I am the somewhat reluctant ringleader of our motley band of paranormal hoodlums, I found myself burying the dread of announcing our arrival, since the reaction to paranormal investigators is profoundly hit or miss. Even prefacing it with "published author" will only get you a cup of coffee if you also happen to have a dollar.

This was decidedly *not* the case at the George and Dragon. I found Keith, the day manager, at a crowded outside table, celebrating the birthday of a friend. I rather sheepishly interrupted while the group tried to come to a consensus on what constituted an authentic punk-rock Mohawk. When queried, I had to concede that an authentic Mohawk was usually quite tall and involved a generous application of Elmer's glue. We were immediately welcomed into the fold and I had to wonder what I was so intimidated by in the first place.

The Office

When the last of the revelers had been shooed away and the bar tabs closed, the pub emptied out and the only people left inside were the three of us, Keith, and his friend Rachel. Keith turned off

The office of the George and Dragon Pub... Katie stood face-to-face with a dark, shadowy apparition here.

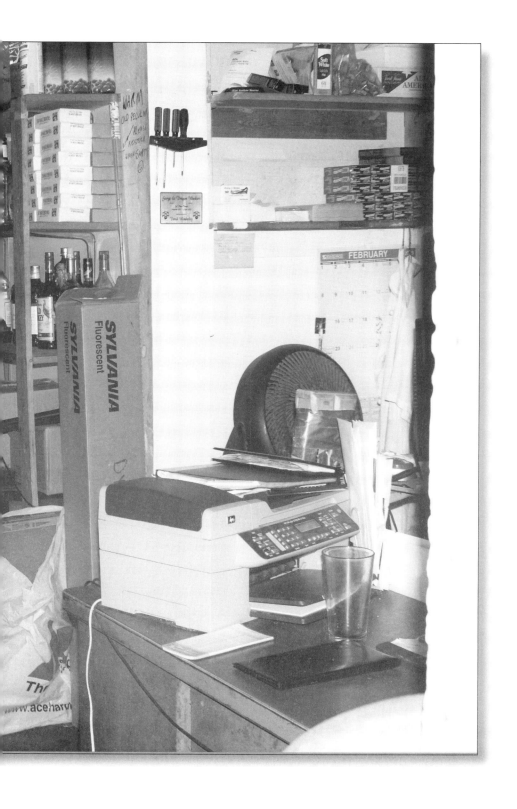

the lights and gave us free reign. The building was completely dark, save for a few small, necessary lights that shared a breaker with the security system. Initially, I wasn't sure where to start since the place is segmented and somewhat compartmentalized, so I decided to follow the path that we were shown on the cursory tour we were given so that we could acclimate and be orientated in the darkness. I walked behind the bar, and turned the corner towards the back. I paused in the doorway of the office to have a look and allow my eyes to adjust to the surroundings in the dark. Normally, my eyes would adjust and I would be able to make out shapes well enough to discern a chair from a table, but after several seconds I realized that I was staring into a chasm of darkness with blurred edges, allowing me only to see the right side of the office, while the left side was completely obscured by a thick, dark haze. I continued to stare at this impenetrably dark cloud and it began to dawn on me that I was not only gazing with confusion into an inexplicable cloud of darkness, but that *it*, too, was gazing back at me.

Filling with a bit of panic, I backed away slowly and continued down the hall. The full impact of that encounter would not hit me until I passed the office a second (and third) time and realized both times that I could clearly see the faint glint of the liquor bottles lining the previously obscured back wall. Was this simply an errant shadow, or could I have just been standing face-to-face with an apparition?

The Kitchen

I continued down the hallway and into the kitchen area. Now, as with any situation that puts you in the dark in a strange place, this dark galley kitchen made my heart beat a bit faster. I dreaded the twenty or so steps it would take to pass through. Fortunately, for this portion of the walk-through, my husband Mikal was nearby snapping photos. While my brain knew I wasn't alone, it couldn't convince my stomach to stop flip-flopping with anxiety. As I ventured forth, the slight comfort that I took in knowing that I was not all by myself in the back of the restaurant quickly morphed into a weighty dread of certainty that I was *not alone*, if you catch my drift.

The feeling in the kitchen area was still and suffocating. At all times, it felt as though there were someone simultaneously in front

The kitchen of the George and Dragon Pub... This is where Katie felt her hair being pulled by unseen hands.

of, next to, and behind me. I finished my walk through the kitchen and exited through the double-doors into a small wait station adjacent to the dining room. I can only liken the severity of the change in atmosphere to walking through a wardrobe and ending up in a completely different parallel world where a goat boy slips you a roofie and a Rastafarian Tilda Swinton rolls up in a pimped-out sleigh wearing an enormous white bathmat and offers you some inedible confection. Okay, perhaps that is a bit of an exaggeration. Nevertheless, the feeling in the air was lighter and significantly less ominous — an indication that we may have just been in the midst of a paranormal event!

EVP

We made individual rounds a few times, recording our own impressions, thoughts, and feelings in our notebooks, but on the last lap of the investigation, we spent some time doing EVP work. We walked through the different rooms, asking the obligatory questions, "Is there anyone here?" and "What is your name?" When we walked into the kitchen for the final pass, I paused and again asked, "Is there anyone here?" As if in direct response to that question, I suddenly felt the gentle touch of fingers against the side of my face, pulling a lock of hair from my securely bound ponytail (not unlike a similar experience described in *Tucson's Most Haunted*). I let out a very Julia Roberts-esque laugh-gasp, as a chill ran down my spine. Clearly there is something to this ghostly business!

The Pub's History

After the walk-through was complete, we sat down again with Keith to find out exactly why this place appears to have a mind and *spirit* of its own. The building that houses the pub has been around for several decades and is the location of the very first Shakey's Pizza in Phoenix. It was during that time someone was gunned down in the restaurant in a fit of jealous rage — not coincidentally, in the exact spot in the kitchen where I felt my hair pulled by the unseen hand.

Although many folks would consider dark shadows and ominous presences enough of an indication that a place is haunted, it is by no means the only activity that occurs in the pub. As it turns out, things have a way of moving about on their own. Pointing to a light hanging above one of the pool tables, Keith gave us the rundown: "The lights over the pool table…I'm surprised they're not moving now. They'll move in a two-foot span towards the wall."

An inspection of the pool table area showed no vents or air-conditioning ducts that would be responsible for the motion of the light. Evidently, the ghosts were a little confused about which light they should be playing with because, as Keith was lamenting the fact that the ghosts were not messing with the lights, an overhead light switched off as if on cue. Now, it could be argued that the light in question was on a timer, but judging by the genuinely uneasy reaction that Keith and Rachel — who both have a much more intimate knowledge of the normal "closing time" goings on — seemed to have in response to the light going out made the incident noteworthy, and that was not to be the last of the shenanigans.

As Keith continued to explain the myriad of activity that has been reported and that he has experienced, he explained to us that the mother of the pub's owners had very recently passed away. He theorized that some of the more recent activity might be caused by her presence. No sooner than he had said that, a printer near the bar began randomly printing register tapes that, upon inspection, contained only the names of the two owners and sons of the deceased. What makes this incident even more compelling is that one of the owners has never logged in to the computer that controls the end-of-day receipt calculations. Visibly unnerved, Keith acknowledged her presence by saying, "hello," and Patrick apologized to the rambunctious spirit for an earlier outburst of profanity he expelled as a reaction to the cash register loudly going haywire. At the time, he didn't realize he was speaking to someone's dead mother.

The list of activity seems endless — a women's restroom has such notable drops in temperature that one's breath can be seen, even in the draining heat of the Arizona summer; the vision of a woman can be seen on real-time security video, seated at a table near the back of the bar; a pay phone rings every night at the same time, though no phone company records show any inbound calls; and there's surveillance video of a potato that maneuvers its way out

The light above this pool table at the George and Dragon Pub has a tendency to swing back and forth of its own volition.

of a bag and floats momentarily before dropping to the ground. Clearly these activities do not fall under the category of "normal" restaurant operations.

What is causing this activity? It has been occurring for several years, with other paranormal groups documenting some pretty phenomenal EVP. One possible explanation is the theory that the bar is built atop sacred ground. It may seem trite, but it's almost impossible to throw a rock in Arizona without hitting ground that is considered sacred by any number of Native American tribes.

In fact, Keith showed us a fenced-off area directly across the street from the pub that is a documented Hopi burial ground. Although unmarked, these parcels of land are, in fact, sacred and should be regarded with reverence and respect. Though a small portion of the area is fenced-off to provide protection, the actual burial ground could extend for miles in the surrounding area, which would put The George and Dragon Pub squarely inside its swirling and spiritually chaotic energy core and make the Pub a not-to-be-missed ghost hunting location. After all, where else can you pair a pint of ale with a plate full of paranormal?

Patrick's Investigation Notes

I've never been to an English pub before. Given that I don't drink, I don't find myself in pubs or bars of any kind unless it is to sing karaoke or play pool, so I have no real point of reference regarding the authenticity of the English Pub experience. However, I will say that if it is not anything like what is found at The George and Dragon Pub in Phoenix, then it should be.

Entering the restaurant and bar, after passing through a patio area complete with heaters for patrons who don't want to freeze to death while having a smoke, you can't help but notice the open and inviting feel to the place. The bar is situated directly across from the entrance, with booths lining the walls and tables filling the space in between. To your right is a separate dining area and to your left, behind a partial partition, are the requisite pool tables and dart boards.

We showed up just before closing time at 2 a.m. and found the crowd inside starting to thin out. The patio, however, was still active

You may want to find a knight-in-shining armor to accompany you when going to this haunted hotspot!

and filled mostly with regular patrons. We spent time chatting with them about various topics and found them to be enormously friendly and eager to welcome newcomers. If a bar can be judged by its patrons, the G and D proved itself to be friendly, welcoming, and boisterous. Sometimes you want to go where everybody may not know your name, but will regale you with bad jokes in a slightly slurred East End accent.

Once the heaters were turned off, we moved inside and hung around in the main area of the pub while the bartenders and night management closed out the registers and performed other various duties. Standing in the room, I couldn't help but feel antsy. Right off the bat the place seemed absolutely alive and brimming with energy. I don't mean energy in some kind of hokey New Age sort of way, but just that electric feeling you get when a place is crowded and there is a lot going on.

Closing activities completed, the lights were turned off and we were able to begin our walk-through. The place was pretty dark. There was some light from monitors and the bathrooms, which shared a breaker with the alarm system and thus could not be turned off without completely compromising the establishment's security. I can see pretty well in the dark and there was enough ambient light around to not kill myself navigating around tables, so I didn't feel the need for a flashlight. This was a good thing, as we generally never bring any. This helps with the mood and the overall focus, but can sometimes be bad on the shins.

Dining Area

My first destination on the walk-through was the separate dining area. When I got to the first available corner, I found myself feeling butterflies in my stomach and my equilibrium started to get a bit wonky. These are both fairly common sensations in a situation involving paranormal activity, so I jotted it down on the floor plan and moved deeper into the room. I was facing the back wall looking at a doorway leading to a set of bathrooms to my right and a doorway to the kitchen to the left. All at once, I felt a massive pressure building around me that hit with the intensity of a punch to the stomach, which is coincidentally where I felt it the most.

Many people know what it is like to be watched by someone else. You just know. Your skin starts to crawl and it makes you acutely uncomfortable. The sense that you are not alone is also very urgent and distinct. I felt both of those things with an intense certainty that the origin of these feelings was the kitchen. Now, it is fair to say that the darkness breeds paranoia and often you get creepy feelings in the dark based on a very well-founded fear of the unknown, in this case someone or something out to do you harm, but I have been in enough pitch-black rooms to know the difference between home-grown crawling paranoia and someone standing six feet to my left who is glaring at me.

I shook off the feeling and moved to the right to the bathrooms. In the alcove separating the bathrooms from the dining room, I felt the distinct sensation of being followed, as well as a more generalized apprehension and anxiety. Entering the women's bathroom did nothing at all to banish these feelings. I moved into the room after stopping at the mirror to lament how fat I am getting and, standing in front of the stalls, I couldn't help but to look over my shoulder. No one was there and there was no movement to base my head turning on, but I couldn't shake the distinct impression that someone was standing next to me. The general feeling of increased pressure around me continued as well. I left the women's bathroom and entered the men's and found nothing out of the ordinary beyond a smell I could have done fairly well without. I only lingered in this room for a short time before moving on.

The Bar Area

I went back to the main bar area and crossed over to the long alcove that housed the pool tables and a second set of bathrooms. Wandering the area, I felt a very claustrophobic, closing-in sensation not too far from the closest pool table. I made my way to the bathrooms on this side and found nothing at all out of the ordinary. From the bathrooms I made my way behind the bar itself and angled myself toward the back kitchen area. Behind the bar, I noticed the closing pressure started to make itself known again. There is a certain density to the air back there that is hard to describe, but it is almost palpable enough to climb like a ladder.

The Kitchen

Heading into the kitchen, I found the darkness back there a bit more oppressive, mostly due to the lack of any real external light. Standing back there and making my way down the narrow hallway of wash sinks and storage racks, I was overwhelmed by the feeling of being followed — *and followed closely*. The feeling moved around a bit depending on my forward motion or my orientation when standing still. It felt very much as if someone was standing right in front of me or right behind me at all times. It did not feel as if *it* were terribly happy or friendly. The whole vibe of the place is distinctly different in the kitchen area. Where the main room and adjoining rooms felt welcoming, the kitchen felt as if you were trespassing in the Prince's forest and how dare you shoot one of the King's deer, Robin Hood?

Moving into the grill area of the kitchen, the feelings began to escalate to full-scale panic. I am not talking about being scared, but rather it felt as if I was on the brink of hyperventilating. The feeling of a presence was still very intense and I could catch flashes of movement around me. If the feeling were a dinosaur, it would be called "Creepasaurus Rex" and it would make you want to leave the area immediately.

I moved into the alcove between the kitchen and the dining area where I had begun my walk-through and found myself to be so dizzy I was in danger of toppling over at any moment. The feeling continued until I was well inside the main bar area. At this point, after a few more walks around the place, we sat down to hear the skinny on the place.

Comparing Notes

Sitting and talking to Keith (the day manager) and Rachel, we lost a good portion of the little light we had all at once. We were sitting there talking, and the light went out. Could have been a burnt-out bulb or some kind of timer, but Keith didn't seem to think so. He and Rachel were fairly alarmed, and I found that to be notable given their reasonably extensive experiences at the location. A little while later, a register tape began to print out on its own...two hours *after* the night crew did their closeout. The numbers on the tape were blank and carried the names of the two current owners, one of whom has not run a register of any kind for quite some time. Several minutes passed and another register tape in a different part of the bar started to print. This one seemed a bit more standard, but the timing of it was alarming all the same.

After all the stories were told and notes were compared, we found that almost all of our reported feelings and experiences were consistent with previously reported activity, which was quite a lot. Throw in the added light and printing anomalies and you have a pretty active location. Keith told us he was sort of disappointed by the more overt occurrences and it was apparently a slow night that night. If that was a slow night, I would like very much to be there when it's busy.

Chapter Seven:

Hotel San Carlos

If you ask anyone in the Phoenix area where to find a ghost, you will invariably be told, "The San Carlos!" The Hotel San Carlos appears to be a haven of paranormal activity, dating as far back as the opening of the hotel, and perhaps even earlier. Prior to becoming the most famous haunted hotel in the Phoenix area, the land upon which the hotel was built was originally Arizona's first schoolhouse. Built in 1874, the schoolhouse was constructed in an area that had allegedly been used by Native Americans to worship the god of learning.

The schoolhouse went through numerous expansions during the several decades it was used in this capacity, but, sadly, all good things come to an end. The school building was condemned in 1916, then sat vacant for several years until Charles Harris purchased the land. Construction of the new hotel began under the architectural prowess of the G. Witecross Ritchie firm.

The hotel had its official grand opening March 20, 1928. At the time, it was the most state-of-the-art hotel in Phoenix, boasting both air-conditioning and elevators. The grandeur of the hotel attracted many of Hollywood's elite, including Mae West, Carole Lombard, and Clark Gable. Of course any facility that attracts the social elite will also attract a fair helping of scandal, and the San Carlos is no exception. Just a few short weeks after the grand opening of this luxury hotel, Arizona residents were greeted by *The Arizona Republic* headline: "Pretty Blond Jumps from San Carlos!" The "pretty blond" in question was Leone Jensen, a young lady who allegedly threw herself from the top of the hotel after learning that her abusive jerk of a boyfriend was also cheating on her, at least according to what was gleaned from the note that was left.

As you may have already surmised, sightings of the ghost of Leone Jensen have been reported with a fair amount of regularity at the hotel, but she is by no means the only ghost that is reportedly seen. Alongside the sightings of the deceased Leone Jensen, there are also reports of the ghost of a young girl that can be seen crying. Although "little girl ghosts" are often the ubiquitous stock footage of paranormal activity, there may be some validity to these reports based not only on the fact that this hotel is built upon the old schoolhouse site (in fact, the original well for the schoolhouse is still accessible in the hotel's basement), but that there was also a flu outbreak that claimed the lives of many of the local children in 1918. Interestingly, there have also been others who have leapt — or been pushed — to their death from the San Carlos, although you certainly won't hear that topic come up in casual conversation at the hotel.

Numerous paranormal investigations have been performed within the hotel, including a 2001 investigation that we took part in with the Pima College Paranormal Investigation Group led by Bill Everist.

Oddly, the San Carlos tends to be a bit wishy-washy when it comes to discussing their paranormal activity. During our research for our first book, *Scare-Izona: A Travel Guide to Arizona's Spookiest Spots*, we were politely dismissed when we asked if they would like to be featured in our book, indicating that they were no longer interested in promoting the idea that they are haunted. Instead they preferred to focus on the link to Hollywood and the many stars that have passed through the doors of the San Carlos. That is certainly a fair enough statement, and it might have actually held the teeniest bit of accuracy had they not then gone on to host the very first Haunted Con in September 2008, featuring the likes of Chip Coffey and John Zaffis, whose lectures and presentations are entertaining, informative, and DECIDEDLY paranormal.

Perhaps the hotel has decided to embrace its ghosts after all?

The Hotel San Carlos... Several people have "jumped" at the chance to haunt this historic Phoenix hotel.

Chapter Eight:

Arizona Museum of Natural History

Katie's Investigation Notes

I am a huge sucker for museums, so when I got in touch with Alice Jung at the Arizona Museum of Natural History and she said, "We've got ghosts," I couldn't get myself there fast enough to check it out. We arrived at the museum at 8 p.m. on a Friday and were greeted by Alice and her associate, Michael Ramos, both of whom have had experiences in the museum that left them more than just a little creeped out. Although they were eager to share their experiences with us, we had to take a pass on the ghost stories at the outset so that we could be uncompromised for the sensory replication walk-through. They told us they would wait by the front desk and promptly gave us free reign of the museum.

In attendance for this investigation were the usual suspects — Mikal, Patrick, and I — but we also brought one of our resident "newbies," Mo, along for this ride, a decision that proved to seal the deal about the other-worldly disposition of this museum, but we will get to that a bit later. Normally, during a walk-through of a location, we make every effort not to speak to each other or interact in any way that might compromise our findings, but we still have a hard time not crossing paths or bumping into each other while moving from room to room. Not so in the case of the museum. When we split up, it was easily thirty minutes before I ran into another member of the team — *the place is that big*. Fortunately, the museum had maps available so that we could get the lay of the land

and not end up having to take up with Hohokam Indians because we couldn't find our way back out.

The Prison

I decided to start out in the Territorial Prison section of the museum, which consists of…well, you probably guessed it…a territorial prison. This prison is not a replica. It was an actual working detention facility in Maricopa County prior to being moved into the building and, since the building that houses the museum originally spent time as the police station, the cells were once again put to use to hold all manner of convict and criminal before becoming a very interesting attraction.

I walked through the doorway of the prison and, I have to say, I immediately felt a strong presence. It felt like every cell was occupied and all eyes were directly on me, so — as any normal person would do — I sat down on the floor and started to observe. What caught my attention almost instantly were the very heavy, very deliberate footsteps I heard leading up to the prison. I looked back through the doorway expecting to find another team member or one of the museum folks, but no one was there. Still, the footsteps were so real that I chalked it up to someone having gone into an adjacent room and was simply outside of my field of vision. Add to that the very loud sounds of banging and clanging that followed the sound of the footsteps and I was sure it must be Michael either turning something on or off just in the course of his normal business within the museum. I was absolutely positive.

The Mine

After the footsteps passed by, it became quiet again, save for the consistent but minor knocking and pinging.you might expect from an all-metal room. I sat for a bit longer before I decided to get up and proceed to another room by way of the Lost Dutchman Mine, which can be accessed on the far end of the Territorial Prison. That means you have to enter and walk through the cellblock to get to the entrance of the mine. Okay, no problem. I can do that, right?

A typical cell in the Territorial Prison exhibit housed at the Arizona Museum of Natural History. It's not exactly the Ritz!

The Lost Dutchman Mine consists of a hallway designed to replicate a mineshaft, and the walls contain lighted shelves behind glass that contain mining relics and artifacts. The mine makes several twists and turns before letting you out immediately adjacent to the door of the Territorial Prison. It's just a simple little hallway…a simple little hallway that also happened to give off a very intense and inexplicably formidable vibe. I have never felt more like I was being followed, even when I was being followed. It was a little scary, actually. It also seemed to set the "someone is following me" tone for the remainder of the investigation. I scurried past the next threshold into a room with a giant stone head. I stood admiring the stone head until I felt someone approaching from behind. I turned and looked into the next room — a room dedicated to films made in Arizona — fully expecting to see someone, but, as I had experienced earlier, there was no one there. I stayed a bit longer, but, by the time I had looked over my shoulder three and four times, I decided it was time to move in that direction.

The Gift Shop

I walked the ten or so steps that led me into that area, which also housed the gift shop (a place that I would later find has numerous reports of activity) and I stood still just to see if anything else might keep moving. As I stood silently, I noticed two things. First, I kept hearing movement coming from the gift shop. We were not able to investigate inside the gift shop, but we could plainly see inside the gates and could tell that no one was in there. Second, just as I noticed the noise from the gift shop, I saw movement out of my right eye. It simply looked like a small cloud of white that just made a quick movement, but when I turned my head, it was gone.

I continued throughout the museum, never really able to shake the sensation that someone was intermittently following me. I suppose that could just be leftover from my experience in the prison and the mine. It could also mean that whatever discarnate energy resides in that area decided to keep an eye on the interlopers. Who knows?

Much activity has been reported behind the gates of the museum's gift shop. In fact, these gates were heard rattling during the investigation.

Cretaceous Seas Room

I moved into the other half of the museum, part of which consists of a continuous ramp, between three floors, that takes you through different periods of geological and geographic development. It was a constant struggle for all of us because to keep from getting distracted from the investigation given the amount of interesting information that could be learned from the individual exhibits.

The next place that gave me pause is a room called Cretaceous Seas. The black walls coupled with the enormous, ceiling-suspended sea creatures are designed to give proper perspective to the sheer size of the creatures versus the vastness of the sea — and it certainly does that. What it also possesses is energy similar to that of the Lost Dutchman Mine. I stayed long enough to get the full gestalt of the room and, when it was time to exit, I couldn't have beat feet out

The Lost Dutchman Mine exhibit... Katie felt her hair stand on end as she hurried through the dark tunnel.

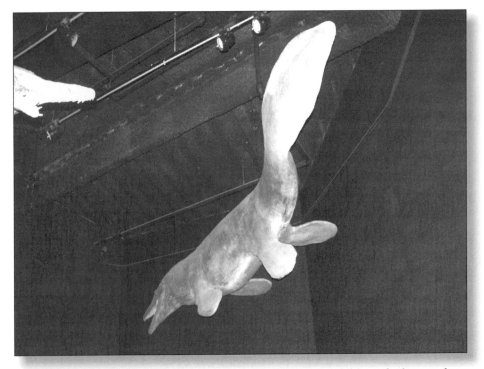

The dark and foreboding room that held the Cretaceous Seas exhibit made the actual sea monsters seem like cuddly kittens by comparison.

of there fast enough. Maybe it was just the sense of being lost and trapped underwater, but it definitely felt stronger than what I might consider "normal" museum energy.

Comparing Notes

Well over an hour later, the team convened at the top level of the museum to go over our findings and compare notes to see if there were any areas where we noted similar sensations. Any overlap in our notes is considered a "hit." The more hits we get, the more successful the sensory replication experiment, and the greater the likelihood that there may be paranormal activity at work. As we began to compare, we noticed that we had probably as close to a one hundred percent hit rate as I have seen on a previous investigation. The areas that we noted were the Territorial Prison, the Lost Dutchman Mine, Arizona in the Movies, Cretaceous Seas, and the Hohokam Village. The Mars exhibit was another area that left individual team members feeling very "watched."

Even as we were comparing notes, we were distracted by noise coming from a stairwell a short distance down the hall. Just to clarify, we were alone in the museum except for Alice and Michael and two cleaning people. We were upstairs while everyone else was downstairs. The noise emanating from the stairwell was that of someone rattling the door handles, as though they may have been stuck on the other side (hmmm, I think there may be a paranormal pun somewhere in that statement) and couldn't get the door open. It was so distracting that both Patrick and Mikal got up to go see what the ruckus was. By the time they got to the door, the rattling had stopped.

When they returned to the group, we continued to go over our individual findings. Patrick indicated that he had gotten some interesting EMF readings in the Hohokam Village (in addition to the physiological indicators) while Mo stated that she had *seen someone* in the Territorial Prison. She said it was a man who walked down the metal steps in the area. Now, it's easy to write something like that off if the person is new to the whole process of investigating, especially given that it is one of the most desired experiences on an investigation outside of some manner of irrefutable proof. However, since she also happens to be my sister, I know that not only is she *not* going to piss on my leg and tell me it's raining, but I also know that she has seen a few apparitions in her life. Even still, experiences like that need to have more evidence to give them substance, and usually that doesn't just fall into your lap. Usually.

Obtaining EVP

After we compared our numerous notes, we decided as a group to go into the areas that gave us the highest number of hits and see if we could capture some EVPs. We went back to the Hohokam Village and sat in the Cave of Time to ask some questions. We started the recorder, identified ourselves, and proceeded to ask a few questions. We were using the EMF detector in tandem with the recorder and, when we asked if anyone was there, it flashed once, per the instructions we indicated — flash once for "yes" and twice for "no." Obviously, if there was nothing there, it wouldn't have flashed at all.

After the EMF meter flashed once, Mikal asked, "Do you want us to be here?" The meter flashed twice — and that was the end of that

The exit sign points to the doors that began shaking and rattling as if someone was locked on the other side. Patrick and Mikal quickly discovered that there was no one there!

EVP session. Not so much out of fear of supernatural retribution, but more out of respect for the reverence of the Native American artifacts and, quite possibly, the spirits that were present.

Our next stop was back to the Territorial Prison. We walked through as a group and asked a few EVP questions. While we were walking through, Mo indicated that, out of her peripheral, she thought she had seen Patrick standing at the foot of the metal stairs, but when she looked towards the corner, the image disappeared. That now makes twice in one evening that Mo saw an apparition in exactly the same spot…very, very intriguing.

The Museum Staff

At this point, we decided that we would now present our sensory replication findings to Alice and Michael who were waiting at the front desk. They were clearly very curious about what we were about to tell them. Before we explained our experiences, Patrick took the opportunity to educate them on our exact methodology just to put our experiences as compared to theirs in the appropriate perspective. We began to share the results of our sensory replication, but there was just so much, I wasn't sure where to start. So, we decided to bring out the big guns right away and tell them about our collective experiences in the Territorial Prison. I explained that as soon as I went into the room, I felt watched, but then I also heard the footsteps and banging, which I attributed to Michael having gone back into that part of the building. Oddly, when I mentioned that, Alice and Michael looked at each other quizzically and then back at me with looks on their faces that already conveyed what they were about to say.

"We've been sitting at this desk the whole time," Alice confirmed.

I just sort of looked back at them with a smile, but I am fairly certain that they weren't as amused by the idea of a stomping, banging ghost as I was. In situations like this, one does have to be cautious and remember that these people have to come back here the next day, so it is always best to tread lightly and delicately when telling someone about your experiences in their haunted location. Just be very matter-of-fact and save the drama for your momma.

We continued to discuss the Territorial Prison, and Mo was especially enthusiastic about having seen an apparition on the metal stairwell. I believe it was at that moment that Alice threw an expletive into the mix. Evidently this wasn't the first time an apparition was seen in *that* location. Alice compared our experience to what a previous investigator had described:

"I've heard stories of things that have been in the jail, and there was another ghost hunter here about ten years ago who saw an apparition or something coming down the stairs. He had spent the night in the jail and at some point saw this figure coming down the stairs… He couldn't see a face, but had the feeling that [the figure] was just disgusted that he was in there. He kind of spoke to it and it turned — I'm telling you from the newspaper article that was written that everyone denies, but I found it on file — and looked at him as best as you can look at someone without a face and then walked off into the museum out into this direction."

It was at the base of this staircase in the Territorial Prison exhibit that Mo locked eyes with the ghostly man. Was this the same phantom that frightened another investigator many years ago?

The Hohokam Village exhibit boasts an unusually high and oddly intermittent EMF level.
Some people have claimed to see the ghost of an Indian woman here.

Alice pointed to the area behind the desk, which happens to be the room dedicated to movies filmed in Arizona, and is also adjacent to the Territorial Prison. Wow... I'm going to call that a direct hit.

We also discussed the Hohokam Village area, which gave all of us pause during our walk-through, and Alice mentioned that not only has she felt a bit uncomfortable in that area, but other museum employees and the late-night cleaning crew have all been very uncomfortable in that area, as well. She further explained:

"There are stories told about the southwest gallery where the Hohokam Village is. I've heard — and this is all just told to me secondhand. I don't spend a lot of time back there. I've gotten freaked out — of a Native American woman kind of hovering over the houses back there. A couple of the cleaning crews have quit over time because they don't want to be back there. Former curators, especially the history curator, would be frightened. He had weird hours and he'd come in at ten in the morning and stay until ten at night, but he would often sense movement back there and go out that back door into the alley at times because it was too intense for him."

The hits just kept coming...

Another major area of activity based on reports is the basement. By the time we reached the basement, I had the beginnings of what would become a splitting headache...perhaps even a migraine. We entered the basement, and I immediately got light-headed and dizzy — not the least bit uncommon in an area with a lot of activity... especially one that is as closed off as the basement of an old building. Feeling very much like I wanted to go back upstairs because I was mortified at the idea of passing out in the basement of a museum, I did just that...go back upstairs, that is. The others stayed downstairs and completed the walk-through of the basement.

Though we didn't get as impressive a set of results in the basement, we still pinpointed some areas that seemed like they might be considered "hotspots." Alice described her experiences in the basement:

"We have stuff happening in the basement down in our offices all the time. Not so much in my office, thank God. [The basement] was the police station when this was originally built — the jail was actually brought here. This is a WPA building built in 1937, and the territorial jail was used as the Mesa City jail until the 1970s when they built the new police station. So, the basement was the police station, the vault down there was the evidence vault, Michael's office and the one directly behind mine — I think that's the wall that has the one-way window — I think that was the interrogation room. I've heard things in that room such as jingling keys, what sounds like chairs being moved across the floor, and boxes being shoved across the floor."

Even Michael has had his own strange experience in the basement.

"One time I had gone downstairs to my office and I was doing what I normally do and the clock on the wall had stopped and I thought the battery must be dead, so I go to the wall and you have to take the clock off the wall to get to the back to get to the battery, and the battery was popped out. There are certainly other possibilities, but that was just weird because I am the second person [here in the morning] and I stayed until 5 p.m., and there was no reason for anybody to go down there, and that battery on that clock is not something that would just fall out. It's very tight. You have to actually pry it out; it doesn't just hang in there very loosely... I felt strange about it... The vibe that I got was that *something* had done that other than [it being] somebody's joke."

This museum is, by far, one of my most favorite investigations in all three of the books for which we have done any investigating. Not only is this museum a fabulous place to hang out with the kids for the afternoon, it houses some of the most interesting artifacts and educational displays in the state...as well as some of the most active ghosts! I highly recommend placing the Arizona Museum of Natural History at the very top of your to-do list. You may not run into Ben Stiller, Robin Williams, or a giant gum-chewing monolith, but if you spend enough time there, you may instead experience a spine-tingling "Fright at the Museum!"

Patrick's Investigation Notes

When you are a paranormal investigator, you visit and tour a variety of different places. From restaurants to hotels to libraries and office buildings, we see a lot of places. Occasionally you get a break from the decommissioned sanitariums and the random ditches where marauders killed a bunch of people and go somewhere that is oddly rare and much more Scooby-Doo than any of the previous locations. We've yet to manage a haunted amusement park (you hear that, Disneyland?), but this time we pulled off the Arizona Museum of Natural History. I cannot speak for the rest of the team, but I was really excited by the change of pace as well as for the opportunity to investigate a real museum.

It is interesting to me that we have not encountered more museums in our years of investigating given how popular they are in movies and horror stories. Occasionally we will go out to small transportation museums or locations that were once private homes or businesses and have become museums by way of preservation, but this is the first major museum we have come across. In all fairness, it should be noted that we stick to investigating haunting phenomena and do not tend to chase awakened mummies or Dracula looking for a magic scepter to undo the vicious screwing he got from Van Helsing back in 1897, so that may count us out as far as Hollywood is concerned. Likewise, we tend to steer clear of the kinds of curses that make T-Rex skeletons chase us around.

Also, many museums have active scientific research going on and the kinds of people who do scientific research tend to be skeptical of the validity of the paranormal as a real science. Of course, that a lot of "investigators" utilize the all-purpose "Ooh, I don't like that room!" and "drink wine coolers while asking a Ouija® board stupid questions" methods does very little to convince them otherwise. When you look at the so-called methodologies employed by some paranormal groups out there, you can't really be all that annoyed by the wrongheaded discrimination we suffer. Some of these people make me not believe in the paranormal and I have been experiencing paranormal activity since I was about eight years old.

So, like I said, this was a nice change. We met Alice and Michael from the museum in the alley and went in through the backdoor. As always, I love being able to go into places the public does not normally get to go. There was nothing particularly notable in the employee-only areas, but I think I just like being able to be back there.

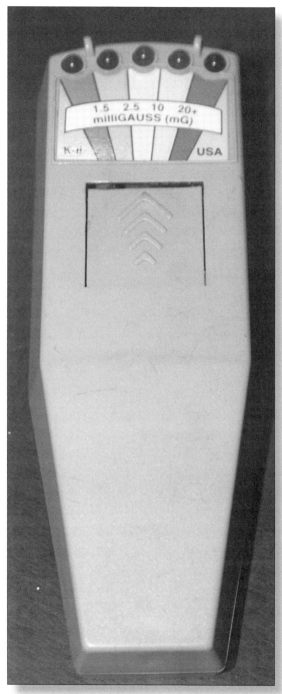

The K2 meter is the red-headed stepchild of paranormal investigation. The brightly colored circus lights make you feel like it will read your fortune, but not until you cram a coin into the slot.

We were shown to the main hall and dropped our stuff behind the information desk. I tried not to gawk at the expansive room, which was dominated by a wooly mammoth fossil cast skeleton.

We divvied up the equipment among the team members. I got the EMF detector, which is pretty standard. I was offered our new K2 EMF detector, but because I think it is both trendy and a bit pretentious, I declined. The thing is the penny loafer of the paranormal world and not for nothing, but I would expect a piece of approved standard equipment to be able to get by without wedging a coin against the button to keep it working. Also, the lights look silly, so I took the EMF detector, Katie took the K2, Mikal took his camera, and Katie's sister Mo, our newest team member and first-time investigator, took the sound recorder.

The museum staff seemed surprised by our meager amount of equipment, but also relieved that we were not strapping unlicensed nuclear accelerators to our backs or wheeling in computer mainframes and enough camera setups to cover a U2 concert. After a bit of general futzing around to sort out which route each of us would take so as not to bump into or scare the daylights out of each other, we set about doing our individual walkthroughs.

The building the museum occupies is very large. This became apparent to me as I took an interesting tunnel into darkness. The tunnel sloped downward and I found myself in a small theater. It did not have any chairs, but rather some railing and an area to mull about. It was the kind of theater you went in during tours to watch an educational video before moving on to the exhibits. In this case, the room was completely dark with only the light from the other room keeping me from racking myself on the railing.

Every time I start a new investigation, especially after it has been awhile since the last one, I worry that I am either not going to find anything or that I will be so worried about not finding anything that I will manufacture a host of butterflies and uneasy feelings that are totally bogus and match up to nothing. For that reason, the first impressions I get are always met with a certain amount of trepidation. The ones I felt in this little theater were no exception; on the other hand, I have also found that when you discard impressions, those will be the ones that are direct hits and then you look like a liar because you did not write them down, but are claiming to have had the same experience as someone else. For that reason, I made sure to write down the butterflies I was experiencing in the theater.

Moving along, I could not see very well because the lights were off. There are people on TV who will tell you that you need to "go dark" to properly investigate. I am not sure why this is, but I suspect it has something to do with the pull cords and key grips dressed in black that are much harder to see as they make it look like collars are being pulled or lamps are moving across the table. Also it helps to sell a Three Stooges-style pratfall as the vicious shoving fury of a disgruntled specter. In reality, it just means that it is more difficult to write things down and to not bang your shins on anything.

Even with the darkness, there was enough light to see some of the exhibits and I found them to be very impressive. I had to really watch myself because I kept reading the little placards and looking at the exhibits rather than paying attention to my walk-through. I used to want to be a paleontologist when I was a kid, so I could not really help it.

Following the progression of the exhibits of various water-dwelling dinosaurs, I came to a room off the main thoroughfare. It was a fairly large but simple room, with a vaulted ceiling and nothing at all on the ground. When you enter, though, especially when it is dark, it is easy to immediately be startled by the two giant model sea monsters hanging from the ceiling. The way you walk in the room, they flank you on either side and they are very creepy. Apparently one of them is of the kind some people think is in Loch Ness. It is actually a really cool display once you get past the initial startle. The problem with the room, though, is that once your breathing returns to normal and you perform the required checks to make sure you don't need to change any undergarments, it still feels really creepy. You don't feel alone and there is a general sense of foreboding at various places in the room. Again, this could have to do with the two monsters hanging above you, but that is hard to support once you have established that they are painted models. It would turn out that everyone else had the same reaction I did, but I am getting ahead of myself.

Continuing through the dinosaur exhibit, I spotted a bathroom and made a pit stop. In the course of my visit, a cleaning person came in and took out the garbage, which made a god-awful banging noise. It occurred to me at this point that any strange noises were going to have to be suspect for the rest of the night. When I left the facilities, I found that the lights had been turned on, which was very good for my shins and sense of well-being, but in this case kind of bad for my attention span. As I continued up the spiral railing, I started getting into different dinosaur exhibits, including two baby Tyrannosaurus fossil casts, that made me feel tiny and insignificant. For a fleeting second, I wished for the sort of excitement that would come with being chased around the place by one of these, but then realized that my health insurance had not started yet.

I cannot say for sure if my general lack of impressions in the main rooms of the dinosaur exhibit had to do with the fact that I was wandering around reading about dinosaurs, but I found that the whole section was pretty much without activity aside from the theater and the sea monster room. I headed upstairs where things started changing from dinosaurs to more of a desert exhibit showing animals found here. The exhibits were interesting, but I have lived in the desert for the majority of my life so there were few surprises to be had by way of the information. Thankfully for my boredom, the reason I was there in the first place kicked in again and I found myself getting a heavy feeling accompanied by a shortness of breath all through the Sonoran Walk and in front of Dinosaur Mountain. I hung out with the live alligator and snapping turtle for a bit and felt more of that heavy feeling. After managing to get the alligator to follow me around as I walked along its little tank, I said goodbye to the upstairs and moved down to the Hohokam Village.

The Desert Culture Room

If there is one thing the museum does well, it is put care and detail into its exhibits. Of course it does many other things well, but I was very impressed by the quality of the exhibits. The Desert Culture Room was a full village complete with a cave and hut houses you can go in. It is kind of surreal on its face because there are models all around and it feels like you are wandering around a wax museum exhibit, but you get to cross the velvet rope and you are doing so without being sucked into the scene with the dude from Gremlins.

This whole area was interesting. Going into the cave it feels like someone is following you pretty much from the moment you enter to the moment you leave. Going to the very back of the thing is something of an endurance trial in terms of creepy feelings. Later, we would all gather in that room to do an EVP session. We asked if whatever it was that was in there wanted us to stay and the EMF flashed twice for no. We obliged as quickly as possible.

In the main room, I found the EMF meter would spike intermittently in the middle of the room. This was curious mostly because it was consistent insofar as the erratic activity is concerned, but was moving around. Because many of the displays are interactive, the museum has all kinds of wires. Even the displays that have no interactive component are well lit, so getting EMF spikes is not at all uncommon or noteworthy in this kind of setting. If the EMF spikes are not static and are moving around the room, then you are dealing with something a bit different, as typical wiring is unable to move around. I came in and out of this room several times and moved the EMF meter around in different spots and kept getting spikes that would hit and then move. Cave aside, these spikes were the only bits of activity of note.

Movies Filmed in Arizona

I moved along to the next section, which turned out to be a display of Arizona and the Movies. The room is circular with movie posters all around the wall and information displays underneath them. There is also a large wagon and Native American dummy next to it that occupy the center of the room, but I was so intent on the posters around the walls that I managed to completely miss that. I was presumably aware of it since I did not break my kneecap on the wagon wheel, but it failed to register altogether. I think it was the somewhat random nature of the posters around the room. Some of them were from movies filmed in Arizona and some were just from movies in general. I couldn't sort out if the "Return of the Jedi" poster was denoting that a portion was filmed here or if whoever put up the posters was a fan. After mulling this over a bit, I remembered I was there to do a professional investigation and returned my focus to that.

I made another circle of the room and found my stomach doing flip-flops in front of the gated entrance to the gift shop. It wasn't right next to it, but rather straight in front of it. A few more circuits proved that was all I was getting, so I moved along. My next stop was the Mars exhibit. I think Mars is pretty cool, but I am not nearly as into that as dinosaurs and movies. I am going to ignore that the last sentence made me sound like I am six and move on. The majority of the exhibits here were interactive and thus not turned on, which in turn meant they were not very distracting, so I was able to focus much better in this room than in some of the others.

The dinosaurs aren't the only thing frightening at the Arizona Museum of Natural History!

Many reports of paranormal activity have centered around this exhibit.

However, all I really got from this room was a sense of apprehension and shortness of breath. As I left this area and went through the faux mining cave, I began to wonder if maybe I had gotten all there was to get here. The mining cave did little to dissuade me from that notion, but then I went to the jail area.

The Jail

The museum was founded in 1977, but the building itself has been around since 1937 and at one time housed the Mesa City Hall, the municipal courts, the city library, and the police and fire departments. As such, the jail cells in the museum are indeed the original holding cells for Mesa and had served as a territorial jail. When you see these cells, it is frankly horrifying to think of people being held in them. Some of the tiny cells offered four bunks. I cannot imagine what sharing such a small space with three other people would be like. I am not claustrophobic, but the lack of space in these things, and the crazy toilet, would be way too much for me to take. Then again I am "soft" and thus do my best to avoid the kinds of things that land people in prison.

While in the jail area, the EMF meter started spiking like crazy. Much like the spikes in the Hohokam Village, the spikes were moving around and they seemed to center on particular cells. There was not any wiring in the cells themselves and the spike locations were far too energetic to have been produced by any sort of single, static power source. Also, that the spikes seemed to jump from one cell to another is further suggestion that something was up — and it wasn't just a little... *it was a lot.*

I was kind of taken back by the EMF results I was getting on this investigation. Most of the time I just carry the thing around and it fails altogether to produce results. To have this much success in different parts of the same location was startling, to say the least. EMF is somewhat controversial in that it is not even a given that the readings we get with the detector have anything at all to do with a ghost. Like everything else at this point in the field, it is sort of a best-guess situation. In this case, I find it hard to explain away the spikes moving around the way they were.

Comparing Notes

At this point, the team convened and compared notes to find that we had quite a lot of crossover, particularly in the jail area and the Hohokam Village. Everyone had strange, not-so-alone feelings in the Hohokam cave and everyone had either EMF spikes in the jail area or they had feelings of not being alone. During the wrap down session with the museum staff, we found that Mo's sighting of a male figure walking down the stairs into the jail area was a replication of previously reported activity. As it turns out, the jail cell activity in particular was replicated pretty much across the board as our experiences tracked closely with reported activity. The sea monster room was also a place where we all agreed.

After this bit of preliminary note sharing, we were asked if we would like to go into the basement to check that out. We agreed and down we went. The basement was basically a group of offices off of a U-shaped hallway. Going down the stairs we got another batch of moving EMF spikes and, upon reaching the bottom of the stairs, a general sense of uneasiness settled into my gut. That was fine and reasonably unobtrusive, but when I got to the back office, I felt a strange buzz on my skin with the uneasiness ramped up to 11 and had enough butterflies in my stomach to achieve liftoff. The whole downstairs area was very off-putting and I am not sure I could successfully work there. Going back up to talk to the staff again, we confirmed the things that we were feeling downstairs were consistent with reported activity. Alice, one of the staffers, was dismayed to learn that the heaviest feelings I got while down there were in her office.

After this last breakdown, we decided to call it a day and let the awesome people who stayed to let us do this go home. On my way out I noticed a display for an American lion and I found myself intrigued. Alice did not miss this and confirmed there had, at one time, been American lions. Apparently there were also American zebra, which was awesome to hear since the zebra is my favorite animal. As we left, I was struck not just by how successful the investigation had been, but also by just how cool of a place the museum was. I really want to go back and just look at the exhibits with all the lights on and without carrying a notebook and a goofy-looking instrument that flashes red at you every so often.

I would highly recommend the Arizona Museum of Natural History as a place to investigate and visit. At 80,000 square feet, there is a lot of real estate to cover and every bit of it is overflowing with awesome and informative exhibits. It is also a great place to go if you want to see about this whole ghost-hunting thing because you can walk around all over and pace yourself. I cannot say it enough… This place is great.

Chapter Nine:

The Domes

    While it is true that often times haunted places tend to look normal and the classic image of the dark, multi-storied house with sharp, jagged edges and a black cat perpetually hissing is nothing more than popular Halloween imagery, sometimes a place just looks creepy. Such is the case with the Domes of Casa Grande, Arizona.

    Built in 1982, the site consisted of dome-like structures and was intended to be used to manufacture circuit boards for everything from wristwatches to computers. Those circuit boards were never manufactured and only one of the structures was ever actually used and only as an office. The four structures, constructed by pouring polyurethane over a balloon and then concrete over that all held up with a metal frame, are all roughly dome-shaped and occupy about ten of the 135 acres that made up the original site. The structures, which call to mind equal parts Native American pit houses and Area 51-style UFO bunkers, were built both for their relatively inexpensive construction and superior insulation. What was once to be a new corporate headquarters fell into disrepair and has remained unused.

    The abandoned site on Thornton Road, not too far from I-8, has not aged well. Over the 27-some odd years since they were built and subsequently abandoned, the structures have started to deteriorate and have fallen victim to vandalism and misuse. Some people believe that some of the uses for the site have been more sinister than others.

Predictably, one of these uses is alleged to be black magic rituals. Tales abound of evil and nefarious goings-on including blood sacrifices of animals. Claims of discarded animal carcasses being found on the ground or hanging from the ceiling often accompany such claims. Speculation also holds that the site has been used in numerous rapes and murders over the years. Given this, one is left to wonder why so many people go out there ghost hunting or parking in its makeshift lovers' lane if there are so many murderers, rapists, and cultists running around. Seriously, is getting your tag up or finding a place to recreate Burning Man important enough to get gutted or raped in some yellow concrete in the desert? I wouldn't think so. This in turn makes me very dubious of the veracity of any of these claims.

It follows, in most peoples' minds, that if you have voodoo magic, rape, and murder, you are also going to get haunting activity. I mean, why not? The place is creepy, weird looking, empty, and in the middle of nowhere. Why wouldn't it be haunted? Come on, one of the domes is even shaped like a UFO!

The reported activity has been fairly consistent. When visiting the Domes at night, investigators/trespassers/drunken idiots have reported seeing a dark shadowy figure running from dome to dome. Sometimes, apparently under less urgent circumstances, the not-so-elusive dark shadowy figure is seen out for a stroll in the surrounding desert. I suppose you cannot always be running, right?

Accompanying the shadowy figure are reports of whispers being heard in the domes themselves. In some cases, these whispers are female while others are male. There have also been some reports of a female voice screaming, which seems to support the tales of rape — or the tales of rape bolster the interpretation of the sounds heard as screams. Some investigation teams have claimed to capture the above as EVP.

Many visitors describe a very creepy sort of vibration as they are walking around, which is often a companion to the whispering voices. That makes a certain amount of sense, especially when you consider that the floor and ceiling are made of the same material, and the structure was built around a balloon and some metal framework. This seems like the sort of construction that might lead to vibration from things like walking and talking.

For those people who park at the Domes for a little on-the-sly necking, there are also reports of a tapping sound on the outside of vehicles. Now all the boyfriend has to do is go and check it out and tell his girl to wait for him in the car and not get out for anything. Then later, in the morning, the cops will come and let her out of the car and show her that the scraping sound she heard on the roof of the car were his fingers as his lifeless corpse swung over the car — at least that is what a friend of mine told me. Seriously, the girl it happened to told a friend of a friend in college...just like every other urban legend.

Clearly the Domes is a creepy place. Even a visit during the day is enough to elicit the oft reported weird feeling, like something bad is going to happen, and it is not difficult to imagine why. Given the whispered stories of evil and debauchery, and the fact that it is just sitting out there all alone, I would be surprised if there were not any reports of haunting activity. However, if you look at the evidence and think critically about it, the illusion begins to crumble.

Haunting Debunked?

Now, it should be noted that because there is new ownership with an eye to sell (as of 2006 the place is fenced in with posted "No Trespassing" signs), Wailing Bansidhe has not gone there to investigate. The owners have stated intent to prosecute and, given the level of vandalism and theft of equipment that goes on there, it would be hard to blame them. Because we advise against unauthorized entry into a location, we suggest that if you do plan a trip to the Domes you had best either look at it from afar or obtain permission to be there beforehand. At any rate, because we have not been there ourselves, it is impossible to say definitively that the reported activity does or does not go on out there. All I am working with is the reported activity from visitors and, based on those reports, it sounds more than a little fishy.

First of all, most of the stories about the place are unverified, almost urban legend style reports. "I heard from a guy who heard from a guy" does not a credible account make. Anyone can go to a place and say that there were rituals or murders done there. However, there are no clear and credible accounts or *official, documented* records of such crimes occurring at the location, which calls accounts to that effect very much into question.

Second, black magic and witchcraft are catchall, boogeyman culprits for anything that seems weird, creepy, or just not right. I am not going to beat around the bush about it. If you are talking about Satanism, the Anton LaVey Church of Satan brand of Satanism does not worship a particular deity and does not go about performing blood rites or human sacrifices. Satan in this context is a symbolic patron of a hedonistic lifestyle centered on viewing the seven deadly sins as seven indulgences, so it is unlikely that any of these people are going to be doing any black magic rituals. There have been reported cases of true satanic rituals being carried out that were under investigation by law enforcement in both Tucson and Phoenix, but in none of these cases were such rituals carried out in overtly creepy locations with evidence left behind. Therefore, it is unlikely that any sort of Satanist cult has ever used the grounds for their dark purposes, no matter how much the fear mongers in our society insist otherwise.

Other pagan groups are equally unlikely to have practiced black magic at the location, as by and large pagan groups don't do that sort of thing either. Druids in particular would most likely be put off by all the synthetics in the construction. I cannot say definitively that no group has ever gone out to the Domes to perform black magic rituals, but it is highly unlikely. If they did, it is even more unlikely that they had any idea what they were doing. There are a lot of cults in Arizona, but generally they don't go out to places like this to do anything and if they did they would most likely clean up after themselves.

Some paranormal groups that have investigated the area claim that the local authorities have confirmed reports of mutilated animal corpses. I am not sure I believe that, but, playing devil's advocate, even if those reports are true and there absolutely have been found leftover carcasses, there is no evidence to suggest that those carcasses were involved in anything more nefarious than the animal having been eaten. Take a walk in any desert or around any ruined structure and you are going to find discarded, mutilated animal carcasses

— that tends to happen when other animals eat them. Much like Saguaro High School in Scottsdale, it sounds like Satanism and witchcraft are being used to explain something strange without a solid understanding of either of those things.

There have also been no confirmed cases of rapes or murders happening at the Domes. I cannot say that there has never been any rape or murder there, but if there has, it has gone unreported. Given the amount of foot traffic that apparently goes through the place with all the taggers, thieves, fornicators, and vandals, it is hard to believe that no one would have noticed and subsequently reported a rape or murder.

Again, I have to reiterate that I find it very hard to believe that if there is any truth to these stories that people would so readily go out there. I understand the thrill-seeking behavior involved in going somewhere scary — I have, after all, made a career of it. However, if animals are getting sacrificed in one dome and people are being raped and murdered in the next dome, I really do not see people going out there. Of course, it would account for where the rape and murder victims come from, but again, if this were happening all the time, the police would be investigating it regardless of how slow their response time might be. There is no way that crimes of this magnitude would go unreported, and if black magic rituals were going on, the police would have no problem staking out the joint and shipping the perpetrators off to the hoosegow.

A Plausible Explanation

Rape, murder, and Satanism are certainly not requirements for paranormal activity, so discounting these things does not equal refutation of the reports full stop. If you read the other stories in this book, none of the activity sounds particularly unlikely or outrageous and it is not. One thing it is, however, is explainable by other *non-paranormal* means.

For instance, if you have large, abandoned structures out in the middle of nowhere, then another thing you are going to have are transients. If you are outside and you happen to be walking in the desert, finding a bunch of large, well-insulated, and breezy buildings in the middle of nowhere would be extremely attractive. You would almost have to be stupid not to squat there. Shelter from the heat and cold alike, as well as the seclusion to not be rousted by the cops or cranky business owners, is hard to argue with.

Now if you put transient squatters into the domes and then you put drunken idiots traipsing around the place in the dark, what do you suppose the squatters might do? Run from dome to dome to avoid being seen? Maybe go out in the surrounding desert and walk around for the same effect? Maybe if there are two of them, they might whisper to each other that someone is coming and it is time to bounce. Rapid movement out of the domes would certainly cause the less-than-solid structure to vibrate a bit.

When you are living out in the middle of nowhere and the nearest grocery store that you have no money to shop at is across a blistering desert, you are going to have to figure out an alternate food source. The crafty squatter is going to find that food however and wherever he or she can. Even in high desert the plant life is not terribly good for eating, so it follows that the intrepid squatter might capture and kill animals for consumption, but no matter how hungry they might be, they're not going to eat the bones or fur... so that stuff is going to be left over. If there is rope available, you might have hanged the animal to keep other animals from wandering in and eating your dinner out from under you. When you have to beat it because someone is coming, you don't have the time or wherewithal to cut down all of the used-up animal corpses you have hanging around.

Paranormal vs. Not Paranormal

I cannot say for certain that the above scenario is how all this goes down, but it makes more sense than the Domes being a place of unspeakable evil and debauchery. I have no doubt that people go there and do untoward things — that is pretty much undisputed and confirmed — but that there is any element of the mystical or paranormal to it is quite a bit of a stretch. It makes far more sense to assume that this activity is made by live humans than the spirits of dead ones. At the same time, it is much more exciting to think it is a group of tortured and prematurely snuffed out specters telling their story to all who will hear them than to think that the goings-on there are caused by a few homeless people, but it is much less likely. It's more exciting to believe that I broke my toe while kicking a weapon out of an intruder's hand, but in actuality I broke my toe on a door when trying to stop a movie from going off pause. The more we desire for life to be the exciting romp it is in the movies, the more life doggedly insists upon being normal and boring.

Of course, I have not addressed the tapping on the outside of the car. That bit is more difficult to explain, but there are a number of scenarios from transients/friends playing a joke on the car's occupants to the overactive imagination brought on by fear that it is her husband out there with a chainsaw and a pair of tin snips. Any number of things could be causing a tapping sound on the outside of a car and the whole thing may be made up as well. When you have fanciful tales of murder and Satan worship that are fairly obvious lies, it is not at all a stretch to claim that most likely those reports are not authentic on any level as well.

The crux of the issue with the Domes is that it is a creepy place that attracts people who want to misbehave. It also attracts people with a need for what it has to offer. People love spooky stories and embellishing those stories, and once you find yourself at a creepy place with a nefarious, albeit unfounded, history, it is very easy to let your mind wander and turn even the most mundane of occurrences and evidence into something much bigger and more spectacular. It is just human nature at the end of the day. It might seem inconceivable that something so big and creepy would just be another group of cool-looking buildings in the desert and not something much more exciting, but the reality is that more often than not, that is exactly what it is. In the case of the Domes of Casa Grande, that certainly looks to be the case. You never know, though. If you have an extra $750,000, you could buy the place and see for yourself.

Chapter Ten:

Haunted Intersections

When one does a basic search for haunted locations in Phoenix, it appears that the greater Phoenix area has an inordinate number of reportedly haunted intersections. Although this is a bit of lore that could not possibly be substantiated through currently available investigative means, it certainly gives one pause when you consider the fact that Arizona leads the nation in accidents and deaths from motorists "running the red lights." Seriously, Arizona is *number one* when it comes to killing off its own residents through sheer impatience and recklessness. This is nothing to be proud of.

As long as we're on the topic, very little infuriates me more than people speeding down the road, talking on their cell phones, running through the red light, as though they are somehow exempt from traffic laws designed to help people *not* die, while on their way to get groceries. Most days, you can sit and watch three or four cars zip through any given red light…especially during rush hour. It's certainly no wonder that getting home from work is akin to playing Russian roulette and, when you throw bicyclists into the mix, it gets even uglier. Since this book is not called "Why Arizona Drivers Suck," I will close my rant with the following: Hang up your cell phones and DRIVE!!!

The 5th Avenue Ghost

Probably one of the most emotionally compelling reports of a ghost-on-the-go is that of a young girl who appears in and around the area of 5th Avenue between Roosevelt and Fillmore. As the story goes, the little girl was struck and killed by a speeding driver who fled the scene. Since the accident, sightings of this little girl have not only been alleged to occur at the scene of the accident, but in adjacent neighborhoods. It was even reported that as the ambulance was pulling away, the little girl could be seen looking out from the ambulance window, face and hands pressed against the glass as if to say, "Please don't let me die."

The Phantom Child

In a similar report, the intersection of 8th Avenue and Extension Road in Mesa is said to have its own phantom child darting in and out of traffic. This story is similar to the first in that the child is said to have been run-down by a speeding driver who also fled the scene. In this story, though, it is a little boy who appears to be attempting to cross the road, but by the time he reaches the midway point, he simply vanishes into thin air.

Eternally Trapped?

Another report of someone apparently being eternally trapped in the act of being hit by a car occurs from time to time at the intersection of 51st Avenue and Indian School Road. Some people also claim to hear her screaming. Others even go so far as to claim that her discarnate soul has come into their home, knocked things down, and taken a comfortable perch upon their couch. I am also wondering if the reports of the decedent barging into the witness' home and creating a ruckus don't also involve the ingestion of bong water.

A Haunted Intersection?

Not all reports of haunted intersections necessarily involve reports of car-versus-pedestrian accidents. At the intersection of 19th Avenue and Northern, there allegedly once stood a collection of older buildings that had long been abandoned before being torn down. While these buildings were still standing, they were alleged to be the source of a number of spooky sightings. Those who chose to park their cars and throw caution to the wind and trespass onto the property reported hearing the sounds of crying.

Rumors also circulated about murderous goings-on in the basement of the buildings. In any event, those buildings are long gone, but the reports of strange sights and sounds continue.

An Urban Legend?

This next story absolutely REEKS of urban legend. Apparently near the intersection of 55th Avenue and Northern there exists a graveyard where passersby report seeing the occupants of the graves wandering aimlessly throughout the graveyard and beyond. Furthering the urban legend status are the reports that many years ago a group of teenagers were playing around in the cemetery, losing track of one of the kids in their group. Unbeknownst to the group, the terrifying screams they were hearing were that of their friend, who was reported to have met a mysterious and untimely death in the confines of the cemetery, and his body was later found near the grave of his uncle. To this day, anyone who dares to mess around in the cemetery will come face-to-face with the ghost of the teenager, who will then (insert scary crescendo) pester you until you leave.

Although there may be truth to this story, it doesn't sound particularly frightening, since teenagers pester us on a daily basis. I find it rather endearing that if I go walking in this cemetery late at night, I will meet the ghost of a teenager who will then bother me until I leave. Perhaps I will receive a continuous poking in my back followed by the eerie disembodied sounds of "I'm not touching you." Or, will it be more like distant echoes of the teenager following me around, cracking his gum until I have been driven insane and forced out of the graveyard? Perhaps an investigation would need to include a Waylon Jennings CD and hula-ho. Yard work and country music are like Kryptonite to any teenager...living or dead.

Chapter Eleven:

More Haunted Hotspots

The Lost Dutchman Mine and the Superstition Mountains

After a grueling 2,200-mile cross-country move from Pennsylvania to Arizona, one of the first things I can recall my father talking about after arriving in the Wild, Wild West was the legend of the Lost Dutchman Mine. The legend was incredibly intriguing to me as a ten-year-old child suffering from a bad haircut and serious culture shock. I wiled away many hours imagining what it would be like to tell all my friends back home in Armpit, Pennsylvania, how I was now rich beyond belief because I found an old gold mine. It seemed perfectly reasonable to me at the time. The Lost Dutchman Mine is — allegedly — located in the Superstition Mountains, which are located east of Phoenix, near Apache Junction.

According to the legend, there was a man named Jacob Waltz who discovered a huge vein of gold in the Superstition Mountains. The amount of gold in this vein was unlike anything anyone had seen before, or has likely seen since, primarily because nobody seems to be able to find the damn mine. Don't get me wrong, plenty of people have tried to find the mine, but anyone who comes close to finding the location seems to end up deader than a doornail. At least, that is the legend. What seems to support that legend are the vast numbers of people, sometimes entire camps, whose bodies have been discovered to have met some terribly violent end, sometimes without any sign of a struggle. Prospectors check in, but they don't check out... Well, actually they DO, I suppose. That's the whole point.

Not only are the Superstition Mountains synonymous with "get hacked to bits trying to get rich quick," they also seem to be brimming with ghost stories. In fact, with all of the people that are alleged to have died there, it would be unreasonable to think that there aren't one or two or twenty different ghosts milling about, waiting for their chance to scare the daylights out of the next group of unwitting campers. Reports range from Apache ghosts, to giant skeletons, to inter-dimensional tears that allow passage to parallel worlds. Add to that the numerous stone formations, petroglyphs, and rumors of gateways to an underground world, and you have yourself a regular Mall of America, supernatural style.

Honestly, I have never had the intestinal fortitude to visit the Superstition Mountains, mostly because I didn't want to end up like a pincushion full of arrows. To a lesser extent, it would remind me too much of that episode of "The Brady Bunch" where the entire Brady family get locked up in some janky, old-time ghost town jail by an old prospector who makes off with the family station wagon, leaving the Bradys to fend for themselves. I don't remember exactly how the episode ends, but I am sure that apologies were issued and valuable lessons were learned. In any event, I ain't goin' a-prospectin'.

Mystic Paper

Mystic Paper is a fun little scrapbooking store located in historic downtown Mesa and, according to owners Kim and Jennifer, there might just be a ghost or two hanging around. Although Mystic Paper is relatively new to downtown Mesa (and by "new" I mean since 2004), the building that houses this haven of craftiness has been around since 1898.

According to Jennifer, Mystic Paper's resident specter enjoys moving stuff around and occasionally pushing merchandise off of the shelves to hit customers in the head. Obviously this ghost has never had any customer service training. Additional reports claim a number of apparitions that can occasionally be seen engaging in otherworldly craftiness in the business' basement.

Teeter House and Rosson House

In a small house built in 1899 resides a quaint tearoom known as the Teeter House, which is now part of a section of Phoenix known as Heritage Square and alongside it are other buildings that have been restored to their original design and are open for patronage on a daily basis. The house is named in honor of past resident Eliza Teeter, who is said to have lived and died in the building, and who is now also believed to be the cause of numerous odd and otherworldly occurrences. Included in the list of ghostly goings-on are strange smells, eerie whispering — particularly hearing one's name being called — doors that open and close of their own accord, and, of course, the ubiquitous claims of items being thrown about by unseen hands. If you are in the area, stop by for a spot of tea and stir up a spectral spectacle!

While you're there, take a short walk to the Rosson House, a Victorian house built in 1895 — it is rumored to have a ghost or two of its own.

This and following pages: The Teeter House and its neighbor, the Rosson House, are both rumored to have ghostly residents.

Old Spaghetti Factory

The building that is home to the Old Spaghetti Factory was built in the 1920s and, as so many old buildings do, conjures up a host of delicious rumors of ghosts running amok. According to numerous reports, not only have employees claimed to witness the visage of an old train conductor poised dutifully at his post in the vintage trolley that serves as the centerpiece of the restaurant, but it is also rumored that the entire second floor is simply infested with all manner of malevolent manifestation. Add to that another layer of scuttlebutt circulating about an underground train tunnel and a long ago fatal collision, and you have yourself a recipe for an authentic Italian haunting, affordable enough for the whole family to enjoy!

Orpheum Theatre

Is there any old theatre that doesn't have a ghost to boast? I sincerely hope not. This addition to the Vaudevillian ghost roll call is the Orpheum Theatre, located a stone's throw from the Hotel San Carlos in downtown Phoenix. This wonderfully restored old theatre was originally built in 1929, and has lived several lives embracing numerous theatrical incarnations. Perhaps that would explain the number of otherworldly inhabitants reported — through secrets and whispers — to call the Orpheum Theatre home. Among the rumored ghostly shenanigans is a dark, shadowy figure that darts about the aisles in the balcony, after-hours plumbing mishaps, and objects that seem to move about without any corporeal help. Perhaps it is because the show must go on...even into the afterlife.

Trails

This is NOT a sporting goods store. Well, I guess that would depend upon your definition of "sport." We actually ventured into the Trails "department store" on 5th Street in Tempe in the hopes of finding out a bit more about the allegations of ghostly activity. In fact, we just asked point blank if there was a ghost taking residency inside the store. Right away the young lady behind the counter perked up and said, "Yes! Emily!" indicating that the ghost even had a name. I was so excited.

However, before we let her finish her story, we explained that we wanted to investigate the activity for this sweet, sweet book we were writing about ghosts in Phoenix, and we wanted to know as little about it as possible so as not to corrupt our protocols. Her face just froze and she didn't say anything else, except that we would have to go through the corporate office to get clearance to come in and investigate. She gave me a photocopy of a crudely drawn map of the location of the corporate headquarters indicating that it was the "grey building behind the adult boutique shop." It was also deficient of any phone numbers.

Since, by my estimation, that is akin to "Pssst, wanna buy a watch?" I decided not to pursue it any further. I am guessing that it is pretty easy to conjure up an apparition in that environment. Synergistically speaking, the whole is usually greater than the sum of its parts, but I would say — in the case of Trails — the sum of the parts equals exactly the sum of the parts…anyone know of a place that I can get a gross of Redi-whip, right away??? In any event, the rumors still circulate like a bong at a fraternity party, so check it out if you are so inclined.

Point Hilton Tapatio Cliffs

As a paranormal investigator, you just don't come across enough luxury resorts that are allegedly haunted. Most of the time you will find your ghosts hanging out in quaint little historic hotels with delightfully petite little rooms that share a common bathroom with three other delightfully petite rooms. Okay, maybe that is a tiny exaggeration, but you just don't find as many ghosts reported in the presidential suite of the Mandarin Oriental.

However, in the case of the Point Hilton Tapatio Cliffs in Phoenix, there may be a reason to book your family's vacation and do a little ghost hunting on the side. According to reports, a gentleman who was celebrating at a wedding by getting his "drink on" fell over the side of said cliffs to his untimely death. Not only has he reportedly been seen bellying up to the ballroom bar, but he has allegedly been seen in the hotel's boiler room, as well. Now, I don't know the layout of this hotel, but I am entirely unsure as to how the ghost of a wedding guest is now haunting the boiler room. Who knows, but can I get another round of Boilermakers, please?

The Orpheum Theatre may have its own cast of phantoms...

Arizona State University (ASU)

Although there are a few stories originating from numerous areas of ASU, the one that seems to come up the most is the alleged haunting of the Palo Verde East dorm. It has been reported that a girl, possibly a freshman, committed suicide in Room 605. Since then, the ghost of this young girl can be seen in her ubiquitous white dress, walking the halls of the dorm that saw her last day, humming to herself.

There are also reports of a former ASU president (Grady Gammage) who passed away in the building that is now the university's archives building causing some paranormal shenanigans involving strange lights and spectral images.

These are not the only two ghost stories reported at ASU, and ASU is not the only university to report these types of stories. Just about *any* university in the state has a host of ghosts, and those same stories pop up at universities all over the country.

Our Personal Favorites

We would be remiss in our duties as paranormal enthusiasts if we didn't mention a couple of our past favorites in the vicinity:

Monti's La Casa Vieja never disappoints...whether you are stopping by for a bite to eat or a ghost to meet!

Monti's La Casa Vieja

Built in Tempe in 1871, Monti's has seen more history than the town in which it resides. As the longest continuously occupied building in Phoenix, the 11,000-square-foot building has proven its staying power. Many of the former occupants and patrons of the place are intent on proving that, too, as they refuse to leave.

While it has served as everything from a boarding house, warehouse, post office, general store, and just about everything else you can imagine, Monti's is all restaurant now. Serving a robust menu of steakhouse fare, Monti's is no one-trick pony. The food, including a transcendent clam chowder the likes of which you will not find

outside of a coastal town, is topnotch across the board and it is complimented by fascinating décor that celebrates the rich history of the place.

This is not only our favorite place in Phoenix, but it is also one of our favorite places full stop. The layout and provided maps are almost custom made for ghost hunting and the open, welcoming atmosphere invites you to take a look around and ask as many questions as you would like. Owner Michael Monti in particular knows his history and is fascinating to listen to, whether he is telling you family history or reading from the phone book.

When it comes to the paranormal, you will find the offerings here as ample and rewarding as the food. From giggling children around the original courtyard fountain, to banging and shaking stalls in the bathroom, to the cowboy who walks around in full duded-up glory, or the spectral office staff that crunches numbers when no one is manning the adding machine, you will have a great time at Monti's La Casa Vieja. For more detailed information about Monti's, check out *Scare-Izona: A Travel Guide to Arizona's Spookiest Spots* for a full historical breakdown and investigation results.

Casey Moore's Oyster House

Built in 1910 in Tempe, Casey Moore's Oyster House began its life as the home of Mr. and Mrs. William Mouer, apparently in a time before wives had first names. Following their deaths, the house has seen many different incarnations, not the least of which is a 1930s brothel. Even when it made its transition to boarding house, the world's oldest profession apparently kept up its rent.

Tragedy befell an upstairs resident in 1966 when a young woman named Sarah had her life cut short by way of strangulation in her bed. Not much is known about the woman or her murder, and apparently she is intent on keeping what little is known about her from fading from memory. Sarah has chosen not to leave her final place of residence and can be seen walking the halls just outside the door to her former room, as well as manipulating objects in the room and taking out her frustrations on women who come to visit. Add to that the general level of creepiness all throughout the room and the occasional witness reports of people dancing in the room from

Stop by Casey Moore's and say "Hello" to Sarah.

across the street and you have an upstairs well worth checking out.

Even without the paranormal activity upstairs, the restaurant/ bar boasts a good deal of normal activity. A hotspot at night for excited bar goers as well as great place for seafood, Casey Moore's has something to offer everyone. The food is excellent even if the horseradish is best sampled on a dare (it is intense) and the paranormal activity is energetic and prolific. If you are looking to investigate in Phoenix, Casey Moore's is a must visit location. Go on a Friday and Saturday and you can be seated upstairs in Sarah's old room. For more information about Casey Moore's Oyster House, check out our previous effort, *Scare-Izona: A Travel Guide to Arizona's Spookiest Spots*.

Chapter Twelve:

Haunted... Or Not?

The locations in this section are in NO Way haunted! Seriously... We Mean It.

We've been down this "book writing" road a few times now, and it never ceases to amaze us just how many people, despite well-known lore and first-hand experiences, want absolutely nothing to do with anything remotely resembling a paranormal investigation. To those people, anyone interested in the paranormal seems to be regarded as crazy and they prefer to consider themselves absolutely above reproach as well as being considerably smarter than everyone who believes in ghosts.

The people who embrace this attitude exhaust me with their feigned indignance and eye-rolling over something as innocuous as the possibility that a ghost is roaming around. It's not like we intend to write that anyone who inquires about the ghost will receive a free night's stay at the resort or twelve free dinners from your choice of haunted restaurants. Now *that* would be both absurd and untrue. Perhaps if we had a nationally syndicated cable television show, that would make us more attractive? In any event, the locations listed in this section couldn't possibly be *less* haunted than they already are. In fact, the very idea that the following locations have had numerous reports of paranormal activity is preposterous and silly and anyone claiming that these locations are haunted is clearly in need of some sort of intervention.

San Marcos Resort

Listed on the National Registry of Historic Places, the San Marcos Resort opened in 1913 in the city of Chandler. Conceptualized by Dr. Alexander Chandler, the fruition of his dream resulted in an oasis in the desert fit for a king and host to movie stars and presidents. During its almost 100-year existence, it has changed hands only a few times, and it has always endeavored to keep up with the latest advances in luxury, holding steady as one of the state's most extravagant destinations.

Now, rumblings about the darker side of the history of this hotel cannot be found on its website. Allegedly, Dr. Chandler lived in the hotel until 1950 and it is reported that he passed away on the property. It is also alleged that one of his mistresses committed suicide there. As a result, there are now allegations of the ghosts of both of these individuals being seen in the hotel.

Among the other events that certainly *never* occur within the hotel are phone calls being placed to the front desk from extensions that don't exist. Also *never* heard are the disembodied moans from an agonized man. Finally, if you are hoping to see the apparition of a woman at the San Marcos, you are just out of luck, my friends, because that simply *never* happens at this hotel... Ever... Under any circumstances. Capiche?

Chandler High School

Another wonderfully historic building in the city of Chandler is the Chandler High School. Officially dedicated in May 1922, with its first class of graduates commencing in June 1922, Chandler High School's imposing countenance conveys the seriousness of its dedication to providing students with a quality education, unfettered by such dalliances as ghosts and hauntings.

Given the importance of protecting teenagers from the dangers of the world of the supernatural, Chandler High School officially denounces any reports of paranormal activity within its walls. The ridiculousness of the notion that a building that is nearly a century old might have a ghost or two is not even worth acknowledging, and

Chandler High School has absolutely NO paranormal activity. Just ask the teachers and employees who refuse to venture into certain parts of the school unaccompanied.

the very inclination that scores of teachers and staff have had strange experiences in the north end of Old Main and the second floor is asinine. Schools are places for learning, knowledge, and athletic shoe ads. Not ghosts....

Dollars to donuts you can find a few sparkly vampires and horse-sized werewolves, though.

Westward Ho

Another wonderful Phoenix landmark, the Westward Ho opened in 1928 — the same year as the Hotel San Carlos. The list of celebrities who have stayed in this historic hotel read like a "who's who" of Hollywood. It also includes a few presidents — impressive, to say the least. However, like many other buildings of its time, the Westward

Ho fell into disrepair for several decades until it was converted into federally funded housing for senior citizens.

Following a little bird whispering in my ear, I contacted the proprietors of the Westward Ho and very politely asked them about the abundance of ghost stories that circulate regarding this statuesque stone behemoth.

And then I waited for a response.

My only official response was from the nice lady in the rental office who told me that the owners "don't like to talk about that." That's really too bad. Nothing punctuates the relevance of the history of such a grand structure than the idea that some guests love it too much to leave it for the sweet by-and-by.

On that dismissive note, you shall find NO apparitions here. Nor shall you find cold spots. Not even if you are the luckiest person in the world will you find the ethereal image of Marilyn Monroe taking a midnight dip in the swimming pool…because, *officially*, the Westward Ho ain't got NO ghosts.

The Westward Ho officially has no ghosts. Officially. Something tells me the residents might sing a different tune.

Afterword

As it turns out, Phoenix is an interesting place for ghost hunting. There are a lot of places to investigate and the depth of experience is substantial. The attitudes surrounding paranormal investigation are as varied as the sorts of activity and locations. If we were to describe Phoenix as an animal, as far as the paranormal is concerned, we would liken it to the noble duckbilled platypus, which, like Phoenix, is a mishmash of different attributes stuck together to make one unique creature. In this case, instead of having the bill and webbed feet of a duck, the tail of a beaver, the poison sacs and fangs of a snake, and the egg-laying ability of a chicken, Phoenix has many different sorts of activity, locations, and attitudes. Sure, the same could be said of anywhere, but Phoenix just seems to have more of it.

In our years of investigating, we have encountered all kinds of people. Usually when it comes to hauntings and the like, people break down into two groups: people who believe and people who don't believe. Separate from that, there are people who believe, but don't care; believe and really care a lot; people who don't believe and don't care; and people who don't believe and they hate you. There are also people who are entirely on the fence about it.

Odd as it may sound, when dealing with people who own or run haunted establishments, you find a lot more of the people who believe and care and it is generally to be assumed that this attitude derives from the notion that business is often helped by ghost stories. Occasionally you will run into someone who doesn't believe and hates you for even asking, like for instance when you are in a place where there is, say, a pool table with a note attached that claims to be the place of death of a famous person and that said person haunts the establishment, but when you ask the proprietor of said establishment about it, said proprietor acts as if you have suggested that not only was Hitler on the right track, but that he was really made of teddy bear stuffing. Generally, though, people who run haunted businesses are pretty cool about it. As far as Phoenix goes, there is a much wider distribution of attitudes toward this issue than anywhere else we have ever been.

There are a lot of people in Phoenix who are really cool about hauntings and who are very interested in having investigations happen and talking about what goes on there. Some of the nicest and most open people we have encountered while doing this have been in Phoenix. There are many great locations to investigate as well with a great deal of history and activity. Given all you have just read, it should be easy to tell where these locations are.

On the flip side of that coin, there is a preponderance of locations and proprietors who are absolutely not interested at all in having anyone show up to investigate or to even talk about it. Some of these people will politely tell you no, but a goodly portion will act as if you are a criminal or a pedophile who has just shown up applying for a babysitting job. There are others who will tell you that they are trying to downplay their hauntings and decline participation only to host major paranormal events. Some will act as if you are casing the joint to steal everything and still others will give you ridiculous guidelines such as, "Sure you can investigate the restaurant just so long as you do not plan on eating here." Probably the most frustrating of all of these is the dreaded "No, this place is not haunted nor has it ever been reported to be" when you can Google the name and read all about the activity and indeed investigation reports from other investigative groups.

The locations themselves are very diverse as well. In addition to the locations mentioned, you will find that Phoenix has a very high number of street corners that are reported to be haunted. It is difficult to actually investigate any of these since they are street corners and onlookers may get the wrong idea, but the notion that a place could be so haunted even its street corners have activity is pretty cool.

If you are an investigator in Phoenix, you should never find yourself wanting when looking for the next place to investigate. It would be almost impossible for a place like this, with its size and history, to not be teeming with activity, so right off the bat investigating in Phoenix is a good bet. When you add in several really cool people and places, it makes Phoenix's ghost equity rise quite a bit. However, because there are places that are not at all cool with ghost hunting, it is more important than ever that the guidelines for ghost hunting set forth at the beginning of the book be taken to heart. If those guidelines are broken, then more likely than not other places will join the fold of the dubious, sour, and surly.

Ghost hunting is a fun and accessible pursuit, but it can also be very difficult and dangerous if it is done the wrong way — and there is a wrong way when it comes to courtesy and safety. Entering someone's establishment to investigate it is not a sovereign right and the gatekeepers are often only interested in their business's livelihood, which is not at all unreasonable. It is the responsibility of every investigator to conduct themselves with the proper decorum and professionalism to ensure that the awesome location that they have just investigated stays that way for the next group. It only takes one rotten banana to spoil the bunch, and unfortunately there are a lot of rotten bananas out there. If this is kept in mind then maybe some of the less open places in Phoenix may open up and join the reindeer games.

At the end of the day, Phoenix is a great place to investigate. There are a lot of places and a lot of activity to keep you busy. Following what has become something of a grand tradition in the Southwest, Phoenix keeps its history active so you can still take part in it today. And really, in a place named for a mythical bird that rises from the dead, was there ever any wonder?

Appendix

Interview with Andy Rice and WCGAPS!

You know, it's really hard to get to the bottom of exactly where the best haunted places are in Phoenix without talking to the folks who are actually doing the investigating in Phoenix. We spent an afternoon talking with our friends at the West Coast Ghost and Paranormal Society (WCGAPS), and here is what they had to say.

Q: Tell us about West Coast Ghost and Paranormal Society.
Andy: What we do is approach the paranormal investigation as completely professionally as we can. We look at everyone as clients, even though we don't charge anyone, and each case is managed as an individual project. Then we approach it from the scientific point of view. We don't use psychics or mediums because I feel it's the same as personal experience and to me it's hearsay. It can still be useful, but for every one who claims to be, in every thousand, there might be one who actually is, so I don't want to be pointing in the wrong direction.
I believe that when we walk in there, they [the homeowner] believe whatever we tell them, so if I tell them something wrong...you know. I don't want to give them the wrong impression. We go in and we set everything up as a controlled experiment the best way we can. From the command center we send everyone out for audio sessions and we eliminate as much audio and video contamination as possible by knowing where everyone's at and keeping them apart

from each other. If there's a small apartment, we take four people in; if it's the Gadsden [Hotel], we'll take ten to twelve people if we can, because there are so many rooms to do and so much space. Then we do our baselines.

Plus we do twenty to forty hours worth of research going into it, with each investigation. Marianne actually does most of the research, but we even look at seismic activity; what kind of mineral contents are under the ground, what kind of electrical lines, water lines, building codes, air temperature, humidity, any kind of solar flares, geomagnetic activity. I believe it was 1989...a geomagnetic storm from a solar flare came through. Back then everyone didn't have cell phones and stuff, but it shut down Canada's entire telecom system — just from one solar flare. It actually went as far south as Texas. You could see the northern lights there.

If that came through today with all of our cellular and wireless services, we'd be wiped out. Even the small solar flares can give off EMF — different ground content, groundwater hitting certain rock patterns — so we try to look at all that and try to rule out all reasonable first. If you rule out all the reasonable, you are left with either nothing or something that's unreasonable, and then you scrutinize that.

Q: And then when you have what's left, is that what you present to the client?

Andy: Yeah, I mean, if we are able to debunk everything...we look at everything...can we debunk everything? Is it reasonable? Sometimes we are not able to debunk and we don't capture anything, so that's the "inconclusive"...and then sometimes we capture things. Then we bring that before the group; we scrutinize all that and then reach an agreement before we do a reveal to a client to make sure everyone's on the same page.

Q: What kind of background do you come from for doing the research?

Andy: Well, I'm a business analyst, so I have a very analytical mind; Marianne, she was a title examiner for many, many years. A lot of it is a learning situation, you know, and when you do research, we tell people all the time, don't go on your first page of Google results. Find out what search engines are out there — there are hundreds — how each one searches…sometimes it may take you hours and hours and hours to get you to something that leads you to something else. So, over a period of two years, we've collected many different sources plus information centers, libraries, museums — we love information centers in small cities — those people have so many stories, but they are a wealth of knowledge, too.

Q: What made you want to start the group?

Andy: Well, basically I kind of looked around, and there were people here with our philosophy, but I didn't want to wait six months to investigate. One thing that we did with the group when my wife and I started it is that we decided not to charge membership dues. Everyone comes in on a volunteer basis. That way, we have some great people who otherwise wouldn't be able to afford to be with us, so we get it through fundraising, donations, and a lot of OUR MONEY and time, but we came up with a great group of people, and, believe it or not, it was on Craigslist.

Q: Did you have your own paranormal experiences before starting the group?

Andy: That's actually what got me into it about thirteen years ago. I was in college. We were out messing around with a bunch of college kids — five of us in the house — and cussing at something and provoking. We didn't realize what we were doing. I'm from Kentucky, and we were out in this abandoned house we weren't supposed to be in. We were walking down the stairs and I got shoved from behind… If it hadn't been for two big guys down at the front, we all would've tumbled down. So we all ran down the driveway. I'm upset and my back is burning; I lifted my shirt up and I had scratch marks. We knew no one was there because it was all wooden floors up top so you could hear someone, plus we had been through the house, but we were all just playing around then. It is such a rare occasion to happen. Since then I have never encountered anything that negative or demonic, whatever it was.

Q: Have you encountered anything that's equally as tangible, but not necessarily as negative as that?

Andy: As far as being touched? Yes. Touched beyond a doubt? Yes. You have those instances where you question it in your mind. There have been times like in the basement of the Gadsden in the boiler room where we had extreme cold spots. We're talking ten to fifteen degrees difference and the boiler room was extremely tight. Then we heard footsteps coming down the hallway and there is only one way into that basement. We could hear "heel toe, heel toe," so we knew it was boots. It came down and actually went around us in the boiler room. There were three of us in there and it's just really hard to wrap your mind around "you're hearing that, but you can't see anything there," and we caught that on two different audio recorders, plus we had a high8 camera set up in the hallway so you could see there was no one else in there.

Q: Would you say that was the most recent thing that has happened?

Andy: No, the Gadsden we did last summer. Monti's is the only place that we ever declared haunted. A couple of us who were investigating saw a full-body apparition, but we didn't have cameras on that!

Q: What did you see? What did it look like?

Andy: It was a woman…blue, white…. I mean, it was a woman. There was no "see through" or anything like that.

Q: What part of Monti's?

Andy: It was in front at the host stand. We were in the front looking down towards the host stand, we had the IR camera shooting down to the Senator Room, we had a high8 in the Senator Room shooting back, but nothing to get that host stand area. It actually came from what looked like the front door area and, of course, we had all the windows covered and it looked like it went through the bar where we had the Command Center set up. They were having temperature fluctuations in there, and then we caught an EVP of a woman's voice.

Our member Sean is the biggest skeptic when it comes to EVP. He was a sound technician for a theater. He has the $500 headphones and listens to everything, but he was like, "There's no doubt in my mind on that one." On the spectrum it showed up that it was not within voice range, but it was actually a lot higher, so to have all that happen at one time...

Having the windows covered debunked shadow play because the only way it would be able to come in would be from the Hayden Room area and reflect off the glass and back in. We light test a lot of things to see if headlights can cause anything, especially when people say they see shadow figures. We've got a big LED light that we bring out and actually have people set up in different rooms, coming in from different angles, changing the shades around, the blinds, to see if it causes any strange effects. Sometimes it will, sometimes it won't.

(Group Member) Marianne: I was by myself at Command; everyone else was gone in different areas, no one's in the front. I keep hearing a woman talking. I keep hearing a conversation, and I'm like, "No one's there." I'd go out and I'd look and I'd try not to stay too far away from Command, but I'm looking out and there's no one there. I go back and I finally say, "Andy, I can hear a woman!" He goes, "Oh, they're out on Mill Avenue," and I'm like, "They can't be... Mill Avenue's over there between two other sections of the restaurant," so we finally agreed after we had a little discussion....

Andy: We actually went and checked and no one was outside. No one was walking by because I went up there to YELL at people to keep the noise down. Then we had another piece of audio that we got that sounds like the restaurant is just "going"; you could hear plates clanking, music in the background, people having conversations, and laughing and stuff...and, no pun intended, but it was dead quiet that night.

Q: Did you start in Phoenix?

Andy: We started in Phoenix, but we go all over the West Coast — we've done Nevada, New Mexico, Arizona. Recently, after all the media exposure, we've had requests from all over the United States. We even had one in Japan!

Q: All expenses paid, right?

Andy: I wish!

Q: How have you found people in Phoenix to react in terms of talking about their ghost stories and locations? Do you find that people are open about it?

Andy: I would say about eighty percent are pretty open, then there's that other twenty percent. When we first started the group, we had to make phone calls to get into places to do investigations. Now people contact us. Sometimes people are like, "This place isn't haunted." Click.

Marianne: [A haunted location] would be on five or six different websites, you know, not confirmed, and we'd call and explain, "We found this on these websites," and the response would be "Nope. Sorry. We're not."

Q: What would you call your most memorable investigation?

Andy: It would probably be Monti's, but other than that, probably the Cuchillo one we did in New Mexico (referring to the Old Cuchillo Bar).

Q: How did that pan out?

Andy: It went REALLY well! *(Author's Note: Official results pending as of this writing, but feel free to visit www.wcgaps.com for more updated information!)*

Q: Do you ever get scared when you do this?

Andy: I don't. I mean, I run towards it. When everyone else runs away from it, I run towards it.

Q: Is there a difference between ghost hunting and paranormal investigation?

Andy: Of course… Ghost hunting is actually when you go in looking for something, and everything you hear and see you automatically jump to the conclusion that it's a paranormal event. Paranormal investigating is actually going in, doing the investigation, doing research, finding a possible reason for something happening, and going in from an objective point of view rather than a subjective point of view. I think that's the biggest difference. When you are ghost hunting, you are being subjective of everything — *you are looking for the paranormal.* When you look for something, it's like when you get your car back from the mechanic. All of a sudden you hear these noises that are happening and they could have always been there, but now you're looking for it. We've actually had members in the past that we ended up having to let go because everything they saw and did was paranormal, and it just didn't work with our philosophy.

Q: In what direction do you think that paranormal investigation is headed?

Andy: You know, I think especially since TV has caught on with it, there are good sides and bad sides. There is the downside where all these fly-by-night groups came up that give people who are actually trying to take this seriously a bad name, but then again it has opened a lot of doors for people where it's more acceptable. You know, ten years ago it was really cliché to talk about it, and now it's almost a common household thing. Now people can get in touch with other people [interested in the paranormal].

Q: Give us an example of what a typical investigation with your group would consist of?

Andy: We arrive on scene, we have our research, and some [members] of our team know about the activity and some don't because we want to stay as objective as possible. Usually four group members will do the walk-through, and then we'll do a walk-through with the homeowner or business owner to find out [what activity occurs]. Their recollection is usually better in person if they're seeing the place, plus I'll start reading their body language, seeing whether they're lying to me or not because, like a fish story, ghost stories always get bigger as they go. Then we'll go back out after the walk-through, we'll discuss where the cameras will get set up and then the rest of the group can be briefed, and then set-up will begin. We'll set up centralized command and then we have all the camera crews set up. Then I'll sit down and do a video interview with people. It's amazing, it works great... You can't believe what people will tell you when you put a camera on them. Once we get everything set up, we'll start doing baselines. During this entire time we're debunking also; we're seeing possible explanations, and then we'll send people out for 20-30 minute audio sessions. Usually we take most of our photographs before and after, and then after the audio sessions and debunking, we come back, tear down, say our "goodbyes" and "thank yous," and then we go back and review.

If we do have any personal experiences, in the past what we've done is we'll have a book in Command Center and you come back, write it down, you don't tell anyone; that way, if two different people have [the same experience] at different times...you know, but now we're going to start doing that with video. We'll have a separate area where people can go with video because sometimes emotions make a large difference and people can't relay emotions on to paper. Then we come back within the next couple weeks, maybe a month [to reveal the results].

Q: Finally, how do you determine if a location is haunted?

Andy: This is what we use to get a determination on what is haunted. A haunted location matches claims and can't be debunked. We consider whether the paranormal activity is residual (like a record player replaying events) or intelligent (active and trying to communicate directly). If we declare a location to have activity, it means that most claims can't be debunked, but there is not enough evidence to claim as haunted. Inconclusive is when claims can't be debunked and there are no experiences or evidence to support the claims. Finally, debunked is when claims have a reasonable explanation for occurring.

Glossary

Apparition: Also referred to as an "Intelligent Haunt," an Apparition is the literal soul of a dead person. The apparition is one of the Big Three of haunting phenomena. Typically manifesting as a silhouette or shadow, the Apparition seems to have actual intelligence. Behavior indicates intention and, in some cases, it can communicate. Will generally have the vague shape of a person, but lacks definition and detail and will have no clothes or objects.

Crisis Apparition: The manifestation of someone recently deceased or in great peril, the Crisis Apparition usually involves people seeing a loved one suddenly, regardless of distance. It is generally believed this is a way of saying goodbye or calling for help.

Electromagnetic Field (EMF): Field of electromagnetic energy around a person or an object that can be generated by any electronic device or power cord, but becomes significant when fields are found where they do not belong. It is believed by many that ghosts and paranormal activity give off higher than normal EMF and one can track strange fluctuations in EMF fields to prove or suggest the presence of something paranormal.

EMF Detector: A device that finds electromagnetic fields and a must have for any investigator. One popular version, made famous by characters on a popular "reality" show, is the K2 meter. It does what any EMF detector does, but you have to put a penny in it to keep it on and sometimes the penny breaks the machine. Any EMF Detector will do — it doesn't have to be one you saw on TV.

Entity: Typically referring to an apparition, it is used interchangeably with any supposed agent of a haunting.

Extra-sensory Perception (ESP): Term coined by J. B. Rhine to refer to a constellation of paranormal abilities including telepathy, clairvoyance, remote viewing, and precognition.

Haunting: Usually referred to as a residual haunting or place memory, this is another of the Big Three. Thought to be a recording of an event on space and time, the haunting is characterized by inanimate objects being represented along with human figures. The figures and objects will do repetitive things and carry no awareness of any kind for their actual surroundings. Unlike an apparition, a haunting appears to have no intelligence of any kind.

Poltergeist: The last of the Big Three, poltergeist is German for "noisy spirit" and is characterized by objects moving around the room. Common belief holds that this is not a ghost at all, but rather the unconscious efforts of a human agent through PK (psychokinetic) ability. Certainly the most popular and dynamic of all of the kinds of activity, the poltergeist tends to occur around people in times of stress or emotional turmoil. It is very common in adolescents.

Psychokinesis (PK): What was once commonly known as telekinesis, this is the ability to manipulate objects with one's mind. This can be what is known as macro or micro PK. Macro is the more overt sort in which the subject consciously or unconsciously manipulates things in such a way as to move an object across a table or to bend a spoon. Micro includes much smaller manipulations such as psychic surgery or making one's heart stop with using the mind.

Psychometric Sensitivity: The ability purported by some psychics to gain images or information by touching an object. Seen often in television and movies, this ability can sometimes provide a vehicle for faking psychic awareness after someone has read newspaper articles on the wall of a place and then regurgitates as fact after touching some item with seeming importance. This may well be a legitimate ability but should be met with a decent helping of skepticism and scrutiny.

Remote Viewing: A form of ESP in which a subject attempts to mentally see through another's eyes. This was tested and used extensively by the CIA to aid in espionage and hostage retrieval, but the program has been shut down for some time.

Stigmatized Property: A property where a murder, suicide, or heinous crime has occurred. Reports of haunting phenomena fall into this category as well. Some locations are reluctant to share their stories with investigators for fear of a property being stigmatized. This usually affects just private homes, but some business owners also feel that it would be bad for business if word got out of the alleged activity. This can stem from religious beliefs, a complete unawareness of the current popularity of paranormal investigation, a mistaken notion that ghost hunters are little more than thieves looking to case a joint, or a combination of all of those.

Vortex of Energy: Used often by psychics, this somewhat questionable designation denotes a mass of energy centering around one particular spot; often times it is nothing but unsubstantiated hornswaggle. Very popular in movies and TV, this allows for a dynamic device to explain why a place is experiencing events only through massive amounts of CGI (Computer Generated Images) and when using an "ancient Native American burial ground" is deemed inappropriate or has already been used in seventeen movies earlier in the year. It can also bring vampires to Southern California towns when referred to as "a hellmouth."

References

www.wailingbansidhe.com
www.windbridge.org
www.georgeanddragonpub.net
www.azmnh.org
www.hotelsancarlos.com
www.mysticpaper.com
www.theteeterhouse.com
www.rossonhousemuseum.org
www.friendsoftheorpheumtheatre.org
www.montis.com
www.caseymoores.com
www.sanmarcosresort.com
www.chandlerhighschool.schoolwires.com
www.eastvalleytribune.com

Index